D0909286

THE
FIFTH REPUBLIC

FERDINAND A. HERMENS

2210 a
v c

N O T R E   D A M E   B O O K S

UNIVERSITY OF NOTRE DAME PRESS   •   1960

Copyright 1960

UNIVERSITY OF NOTRE DAME

NOTRE DAME, INDIANA

Library of Congress Catalog Card Number 60-7697

MANUFACTURED IN THE UNITED STATES OF AMERICA

TABLE OF CONTENTS

PREFACE

The Constitution of the Fifth Republic will, if it is successful, mean as much for the reorientation of constitutional thought as it will for the French nation. Since the end of World War I there has been a tendency toward "negative democracy": The weaker a government was the more democratic it was assumed to be. The new French constitution represents an effort to break with this tradition and to give, once again, authority its due.

Yet, a heavy shadow lies over this attempt. The reason is that reform did not, as it did in the United States in 1787, come about as the result of a combination of a coherent intellectual effort with decisive, but free, political action. In France, reform from within proved impossible. The threat of revolution was needed, and when it developed it created new forces, in the army as well as in the country, which it has not been easy to control. General de Gaulle has tried to do so, and has acted decisively for this purpose. However, in order to solve a short-run problem, he has concentrated power in his person to such an extent that the prospects of a truly institutional solution, which is imperative in the long run, seem to recede farther into the background.

What will happen eventually depends in good part on the interpretation of political necessities by France's leaders. An unthinking reaction to the present concentration of power in the executive would mean a return to the old abuses. If, on the other hand, there is a clear realization of the need for a genuine balance between freedom and authority, France will find that domestic tranquility which she has not had for generations; other countries, in their turn, will be encouraged to move away from the path of "negative democracy." Clearly, this is a challenge to political science as well as to practical politics.

The author acknowledges with appreciation the assistance given to him, first and foremost, by Professor Francois Goguel, who read most of the manuscript and made a number of important suggestions. Professors J. B. Duroselle and Maurice Duverger gave information on various aspects of the problem. M. Jacques Fauvet, M. Claude Julien and M. Gilbert Matthieu of the editorial staff of *Le Monde* were helpful in the discussion of detail, as were M. Etienne Weill-Reynal, a frequent contributor to *Le Populaire,* Mme. Pontillon, the secretary of the International Department of the French Socialist Party (S.F.I.O.), and M. Jean Fonteneau of the office of the M.R.P. Their help, of course, does not imply agreement with the contents of this study, for which the author alone is responsible. Mrs. Hermens edited the manuscript, read the proofs, and prepared the Index.

The author also wishes to express his sincere thanks to Relm Foundation for its support.

Cologne, March 8, 1960.   Ferdinand A. Hermens

THE PROBLEM

THE CONSTITUTION OF THE FIFTH REPUBLIC represents the attempt of a people to raise itself above its divisions, and to confront the problems of the present with institutions adequate to this task. It has a chance to succeed, where its predecessors (14 since 1789) failed, in solving the seemingly impossible problem (in France) of reconciling the principle of authority with that of liberty.

This achievement, however, will not be attained automatically. The Gaullist constitution does have its weak points. These are not necessarily relevant in the short run and should, in the long run, be easier to eliminate than those of the Third and Fourth Republics. Still, a solution can be found only if the matter is tackled with what the French call *en connaissance de cause* — with full awareness of its nature.

The crucial question is whether the new constitution represents a stable equilibrium between the political and social forces of the country on the one hand and its political institutions on the other. Where there is such an equilibrium there obtains what Latin American writers call *institucionalismo:* The institutions are decisive in themselves; parties, persons and programs can change within their framework without endangering stability. The opposite is *personalismo:* In that case an existing equilibrium must be maintained by a particular person; it collapses when that person is no longer at the helm.

The question arises whether the new institutions are not so closely tailored to the towering figure of Charles de Gaulle that they would not fit the lesser men who are bound to follow him. Max Weber,[1] the German sociologist, has spoken of a special type of leadership which he calls "charismatic." It means that the leader is credited with unusual, and at times superhuman, qualities. He can count upon a willing following where others would be doomed to futility, or would have to resort to coercion. Such leadership is, however, essentially unstable. The leader himself may, in the wear and tear of day by day decisions, lose his "charisma." If he retains it, it is yet of such a personal nature that it cannot be automatically transferred to a successor. Therefore, the foundations of any edifice resting upon "charismatic" leadership lack the promise of permanent solidity. Weber adds, however, that the transition from the "charismatic" to the institutional is possible; he mentions that democratic elections are one of the devices with the help of which this change can be accomplished. We shall see below that, while in the case of the Fifth Republic, the electoral process may not be able to perform that task by itself, it can easily do so if supplemented by a few modifications in the institutional setup; all but one or two of them could be brought about without a formal change of the constitution. The good sense which French leaders demonstrated when they avoided a civil war in May, 1958, might well prove adequate in guiding them in the practical adjustments to a more normal situation.

THE BACKGROUND

WHATEVER RESERVATIONS MAY APPEAR indicated in regard to the Constitution of the Fifth Republic must be viewed against its background. If the swing of the pendulum has gone a little far in one direction the reason is that it had gone very much too far in the other.

This does not mean that the shortcomings of the Fourth Republic cannot be exaggerated. Certain representatives of the extreme Right have argued as if everything about what they termed *le système* (in a manner which recalls the way in which the Nazis before 1933 denounced *Das System* in Germany) was rotten; nothing had been accomplished and the "men of the system" were, without exception, tarnished by it. These contentions might be countered with an enumeration of the tasks awaiting France after the Liberation which Michel Debré made in 1944:[2] The country needed a biological renovation, based upon an increased birth rate, a renewed dynamism in the economic field, and to cap it all, a political rejuvenation. What has been accomplished in the first two fields is substantial; it is, with all its limitations,[3] a great deal more than even the optimists dared expect in 1944.

The Fourth Republic's failure in regard to political renovation (and to the fields depending upon it) is all the more striking. Every one of its leading statesmen has expressed his exasperation with the kind of institutions under which he tried to work, and too often was

3

not able to work. The two Presidents of the Republic, Vincent Auriol, a Socialist, and René Coty, a Conservative, have spoken in virtually the same terms of anguish. So have practically all prime ministers, party leaders, and outside analysts. An all but general consensus on the subject is expressed in the title which Hubert Beuve-Méry, the publisher of the (left of center) daily, *Le Monde,* gave to a little book containing his major articles on the constitutional crisis: "The Suicide of the Fourth Republic."[4] Former Prime Minister Mendès-France, who was to become the intellectual leader of that section of the democratic Left which opposed the new constitution, had this to say in the speech in which he opposed General de Gaulle's confirmation as Prime Minister: "The Fourth Republic perishes of its own faults. This regime disappears because it has not known how to solve the problems with which it found itself confronted."[5] Mendès-France added that, while these tasks were large, the Republic did have the material means with which to tackle them. It just did not manage to use these means effectively; the implication is that it was not organized to do so. Mendès-France and his friends did not advocate a resuscitation of the dead body of the Fourth Republic; they called for a Constituent Assembly which was to draw up a new constitution, rather than to have this task entrusted to General de Gaulle.

The political weaknesses which these men had in mind were not limited to those of the Fourth Republic (1946-1958); they had begun to impress their mark on French political life during the Third (1870-1940). In both cases the parliamentary system was in use. There was a head of the state, the President of the Republic, whose functions were basically the same as those of an English or Scandinavian monarch. He symbolized the unity of the country, and whenever there was a gap in the country's political system (as when a new prime minister had to be selected) he tried to fill it.

In all political matters the President was to possess "influence" rather than "power." Power was to be in the hands of a prime minister (called "President of the Council") and his cabinet. The government, in turn, depended upon the support of a parliamentary majority. A new cabinet would begin its career by requesting a vote of confidence, and usually obtained it. Subsequently, it could be overthrown both by a vote of censure — the term itself was not used at that time — and by the rejection of a measure deemed an essential part of its program.

During its 70 years the Third Republic saw 106 cabinets with an average duration of a little less than eight months. The Fourth Republic, beginning officially with Léon Blum's cabinet of December, 1946, reached its twentieth when Charles de Gaulle became Prime Minister on June 1, 1958. To most observers it will appear obvious that this frequent change of the executive is all that is needed to explain the weakness of both the Third and the Fourth Republic. As the the author of No. 62 of *The Federalist*[6] stated: "To trace the mischievous effects of a mutable government, would fill a volume. I will hint a few only, each of which will be perceived to be the source of innumerable others."

In France no government could embark upon a coherent policy when its defeat was possible within a matter of months, if not of weeks and days. Little crises were certain to occur before the final, and fatal, one was reached. As a result, the ministers spent more time patching up differences among themselves, and with their parliamentary supporters, than they could spend on planning and executing policy. Long-term considerations were sacrificed to short-term ones; a patchwork of day by day adjustments became a substitute for policy.

It has been said, however, that the effects of this ministerial instability were more apparent than real. Several members of one cabinet might appear in its successor; certain key positions, such as that of the Ministry of Foreign Affairs, were held by the same person for years. Such longevity did not, however, confer any power of decision. When the cabinet as a whole was weak every one of its members was weak in his particular field; he found himself unable to initiate decisive changes no matter how badly they might be needed. There were exceptions to this rule, as in the case of the policy of European economic integration and military co-operation pursued after the Second World War.[7] Even in this case there occurred the jolting, if temporary, setback of the rejection of the European Defense Community by the French National Assembly in 1954. The over-all picture, at any rate, represented a type of "stability" which bordered on stagnation; the French called it *immobilisme*.[8]

Contrary to a widely held opinion, the work done by an excellent civil service could not fill the vacuum which had opened in the sphere of government. The area of political decisions is one thing, and the bureaucratic routine something else again. Political scientists, from Aristotle[9] to Harold Laski[10] have discoursed on "the limitations of the expert." In the French case decision-making by bureaucrats and military men showed two typical drawbacks: There was a tendency to a traditionalism which stuck to old goals and old methods where a change was imperative; witness the hidebound policy of the Maginot Line after the First World War[11] or dogged attempts after the Second to hang on to the old colonial policy. In addition, these specialists had difficulty seeing "the big picture"; they saw only their immediate problems and failed to realize what, for example, expensive colonial wars meant for the French economy, or what a spectacular type of military action might do to French foreign policy.

Events in North Africa demonstrate what is bound to happen when decisions are made where they should not be made. Thus, in 1952, the newly appointed French Resident Minister in Tunisia, M. de Hautecloque, arrested on his own authority the entire Tunisian government with which some of his superiors in Paris were trying to negotiate. In 1953 certain French functionaries of lower rank in Morocco arrested the Sultan and replaced him with an old man without authority. This time the Resident Minister was absent and, of course, Paris had not been informed. There followed, in 1956, the capture of the Moroccan plane which carried Algerian rebel leaders to a meeting in Tunis which had been encouraged by certain members of the French government. The final stroke was the bombing, early in 1958, of the Tunisian village of Sakhiet which could accomplish little to hamper the Algerian rebels[12] but which was a bad blow to French foreign policy. In all of these cases civil servants or military men had made the decision without government authorization. Yet, the government was so weak that it felt it necessary to endorse what had been done. The inevitable result was a progressive erosion of authority. When, in May, 1958, military insubordination became general this was but the end result of a long drawn-out process.

THE BLAME: THE ELITE AND THE PEOPLE.

The blame for France's political instability has frequently been placed on the nation's "political class," whether it was directed specifically against the men at the top (the actual or potential members of the various governments) or against the rank and file of the deputies and the senators.

Actually, what was wrong with the higher echelon of the French political elite was less a moral deficiency on the part of the individuals involved (although, of course, such deficiencies existed) than the impossible situation with which they found themselves confronted. President Coty, who knew the wrangling among his country's leaders firsthand, felt bound to come to their assistance, and concluded: "I affirm that, taken together, their value yields in nothing to that of the political personnel of other countries."[13] On a previous occasion he had drawn attention to an elementary, but rarely noticed, aspect of French political life when he said: "In the course of their ephemeral existence, the successive chiefs of government have unceasingly, and for any reason, seen their confidence and authority questioned by those who invested them. Day after day, they are tormented and harassed until they are morally and physically exhausted."[14] At times it has, in fact, been said that a particular prime minister surrendered without a serious fight because he was physically unable to carry on.

The tormentors of France's top political elite were, of course, the rank and file of the deputies and senators. Were they to blame? They have been subjected to scorn and criticism since the early days of the Third Republic, whether this was done with the cultured irony of a Robert de Jouvenel[15] or the bitter, if at times brilliant, invective of a Charles Maurras or a Léon Daudet.[16] Certain *moeurs parlementaires* — "parliamentary manners"— developed, and the term is used with overtones indicating that these manners were bad. French deputies and senators seemed determined to be the supreme rulers of their country. Nothing jolted them so much as the specter of a reasonably strong and stable government which would have reduced the vast majority of them to the role of mere "back-benchers." Even for the members of the British House of Commons this role is a burden to be borne rather than a concession to political necessity willingly made; every now and then the grumbling of the back-benchers assumes the dimensions of a would-be revolt. The rank and file of the French senators and deputies took to the task of keeping governments weak, and themselves strong, like a duck takes to the water. As long as governments changed frequently, there was a chance for additional members of the two parliamentary bodies to become prime minister. Their days of glory might be short but they would, for the rest of their lives, be called *"Monsieur le Président."* If the number of those who could reach the top did not exceed a couple of dozen, the number of those who might become ministers went into the hundreds. When the Fourth Republic reached its midway mark, André Siegfried[17] counted 350 living ministers and ex-ministers. Some of them had been in office for only a few weeks, but they remained *"Monsieur le Ministre."* When new elections approached that title proved quite a help; a deputy or senator not able to exhibit it considered himself a political failure, and his voters might share his opinion.

It was small wonder, then, that the very formation of a new cabinet implied a declaration of open season upon its members. The disgruntled were likely to include ministers who wanted better positions, or who simply felt that they needed reinsurance with possible future chiefs of government. The situation caused two American observers,[18] who tried to analyze the "rules of the game" characteristic of French parliamentary life, to state the more important ones as "The Reign of the Ego," "The Reign of Self-Interest," and "In Politics All Men Are Wolves."

The social analyst, of course, will not readily assign the responsibility for such developments to individuals. Whenever a large number of people who do not constitute a "negative selection," behave in a manner which deviates substantially from generally accepted standards, the ultimate cause cannot lie in a sum of individual deficiencies. Even the severest critics of the political elite of the Third and Fourth Republics seemed to be aware of this fact. They would, at times, repeat what Charles Maurras said, quoting from a pretender to the French throne whose views he had inspired: *"Les institutions ont corrompu les hommes"*—"The institutions have corrupted the men." This applies also to the Gaullist criticism of the Fourth Republic. The existing "political class" was severely condemned, but General de Gaulle stated repeatedly that there were "men of high value" among the Republican leaders. Michel Debré argued similarly when, during the dying days of the Fourth Republic, he wrote a brilliant and bitter book entitled *Ces princes qui nous gouvernent*[19] —"These Princes Who Govern Us." In his words:

> ... the behavior of leaders is in part a function of institutions. A particular form of the state, a particular form of government, attract good men and educate them. Other forms will repel them or handicap them, and thus deliver the direction of society to less good elements. Little is needed to deter a man from entering a career. Little is needed to cause the good sides of a man to prevail over the bad ones.[20]

ARE THE PEOPLE TO BLAME?

If the political elite of the Third and Fourth Republics are not to blame the question arises whether the people themselves, who elected and reelected this elite, are responsible. This issue has been discussed on a previous occasion;[21] suffice it to say that what the millions of voters do who constitute a nation is not simply a result of their personal predilections. They must be organized into groups capable of acting; the many "private" opinions must be crystallized into a reasonably clear "public" opinion. In this connection much depends on the methods of organization and crystallization used. Alexander Hamilton[22] drew our attention to the fact that, where democratic government becomes unstable, the result is not unlikely to be found in "improper channels" of government; of these, as has been pointed out so frequently, France has had more than her share.

Charges involving an entire nation appear better founded when they refer to its internal, in particular social, divisions. Such divisions exist everywhere, however, and in some countries they go deeper than in France without leading to politically disruptive results. James Madison, in No. 10 of *The Federalist,* has presented us with the classical analysis of the problem. He was as vigorous as anyone in emphasizing the existence of divisions, in particular of those based on economic interests. He made it clear, however, that social divisions did not have the last word; it was up to "a well constructed Union," meaning to the properly devised institutions of a "representative republic" (assisted in this task by the large size of the country which most other analysts considered a drawback), to overcome these divisions — in his words, "to break and control the violence of faction."[23] There were prominent men who denied that the task could be solved. Josiah Tucker had this to say:

> The mutual antipathies and clashing interests of the Americans, their difference of governments, habitudes, and manners, indicate that they will have no centre of union and no common interest. They never can be united into one compact empire under any species of government whatever; a dis-united people till the end of time, suspicious and distrustful of each other, they will be divided and subdivided into little commonwealths or princi-palities, according to natural boundaries, by great bays of the sea, and by vast rivers, lakes, and ridges of mountains.[24]

Fiske, from whom this quotation is taken, adds that "Such were the views of a liberal-minded philosopher who bore us no ill-will."[25] Tucker proved wrong in regard to the United States, and, turning to France, the time has come to ponder what Walter Lippmann expressed in these words:

> A few years ago I would have supposed that the reason the governments are so weak is that the people have become divided by the totalitarian move-ments. There is no doubt about the terrible mischief of movements which do not recognize the amenities necessary to a people living under the same constitution.
> But I now think it truer and more significant to say that it is the weak-ness of the democratic governments which is perpetuating and emphasizing the division of these countries into two irreconcilable nations.[26]

THE EXPLANATION: THE THIRD REPUBLIC

Our reference to the concrete factors associated with the weakness of French governments can be brief. So far as the Third Republic is concerned, Walter Bagehot had this to say in his introduction to the second edition of *The English Consitution:*

> ... the present policy of France is not a copy of the whole effective part of the British Constitution, but only of a part of it. By our Constitution,

nominally the Queen, but really the Prime Minister, has the power of dissolving the Assembly. But M. Thiers [who was then chief of the French executive] has no such power; and therefore, under ordinary circumstances, I believe, the policy would soon become unmanageable. The result would be, as I have tried to explain, that the Assembly would be always changing its Ministry, that having no reason to fear the penalty which that change so often brings in England, they would be ready to make it once a month. Caprice is the characteristic vice of miscellaneous Assemblies, and without some check their selection would be unceasingly mutable.[27]

This was written in 1872, three years before the constitutional laws of the Third Republic were adopted. Bagehot's remarks are significant not only in regard to the right of dissolution, but also in regard to the fact that the defects of political institutions can, for a time, be offset by a strong personality. In 1872 Adolphe Thiers seemed indispensable, and he assumed tasks which few others could have undertaken: he effected the transition from war to peace; he suppressed (if rather severely) the Paris uprising; he arranged for the speedy payment of the war indemnity to Germany, and restored the country's faith in itself. As soon as he was no longer indispensable, the National Assembly turned against him. Like so many of his successors he had to resign without being able to call for new elections and to give the people a chance to decide whether they wanted him or not.

Actually, the constitutional laws of 1875 did contain a right of dissolution. Its use was, however, tied to the consent of the Senate, which tended to weaken it.[28] It was rendered practically impossible by the events of 1877. The President of the Republic, Marshal MacMahon, forced the Prime Minister, Jules Simon, to resign although he had the support of the republican majority. The monarchist leader, the Duc de Broglie, was appointed Prime Minister and the Chamber was dissolved. This action complied with the letter of the constitution but it constituted a flagrant violation of its spirit. According to the logic of parliamentary government, the right of dissolution is a weapon in the hands of the prime minister, intended to make it possible for him to confront the majority with the choice between supporting him and facing the electorate. In France there was, in 1877, no conflict between prime minister and majority. The dissolution constituted, in fact, an attack on the electorate's decision in favor of the republicans.

What happened afterwards should have made it clear, however, that if elections are held under a majority system of voting, the right of parliamentary dissolution carries the penalty for its abuse within itself. In 1877 the republicans united behind common candidates and regained their majority. During the campaign, Léon Gambetta had warned MacMahon: "When France will have made its sovereign voice heard, make no mistake, you will have to submit or you will have to resign!" After the new Chamber assembled, MacMahon first "submitted" by appointing a republican prime minister, and eventually "resigned" when he felt that he could no longer sign the measures submitted to him.

At times it seems, however, that in France political logic exists more in theory than in practice. The French Left allowed itself to be hypnotized by the anti-democratic intentions of MacMahon; it was overlooked that these intentions had suffered a resounding defeat and that this defeat demonstrated the safety of the institution itself. When this interpretation took hold, a profound change came over the French political scene. During the very period which saw the British Parliament become an *intermediate* organ of government, the parliament of France came to feel superior to the people. Its mood was characterized by what Alexander Hamilton[29] expressed in these words:

> The representatives of the people, in a popular Assembly, seem sometimes to fancy that they are the people themselves, and betray strong symptoms of impatience and disgust at the least sign of opposition from any other quarter; as if the exercise of its rights, by either the executive or judiciary, were a breach of their privilege and an outrage to their dignity.

In France, this attitude became the standard of republican orthodoxy. It formed the background against which those "parliamentary manners" were to develop of which people were to complain for a couple of generations; the senators and deputies wanted all the power for themselves without realizing that they could not exercise it effectively. The cornerstone of "government by assembly" was the taboo placed on the right of dissolution. As Maurice Duverger[30] said: "This regime was not to last. The right of dissolution vanished after a first unfortunate use; when it disappeared the entire system was falsified." A long line of writers has expressed the same view, and Karl Loewenstein[31] summed up their observations when he wrote: "The indissoluble parliament was the biggest nail in the coffin of the French republic."

The absence of an effective right of dissolution was, however, not the only institutional shortcoming of the Third Republic. The plurality system of voting was used only once, in 1871, when deputies were elected in the various *départements* at large. There were certain variations afterwards,[32] but it became the rule to have single-member constituencies with two ballots. Wherever, during the first ballot, no candidate obtained an absolute majority of the votes cast (and, at the same time, at least 25 per cent of the total registered vote) there was a second ballot, in which everyone could run again; even new candidates could present themselves, and a simple plurality decided. Of all systems of majority voting, this is the weakest; as French writers have pointed out frequently, it comes closest to P.R. Certainly, where it prevails no two-party system can develop.[33] It is interesting to note that Woodrow Wilson was one of the first to analyze the political effects of this system. In his words:

> The result is, that the multiplication of parties, or rather the multiplication of groups and factions within the larger party lines, from which France naturally suffers overmuch, is directly encouraged. Rival groups are tempted to show their strength on the first ballot in an election, for the purpose of winning or exchanging favor for favor in the second. They lose nothing by failing in the first; they may gain concessions or be more regarded another time by showing a little strength; and rivalry is encouraged, instead of consolidation. France cannot afford to foster factions.[34]

There is still a difference between the type of multiple party system which arises under a second ballot, and the type familiar from the history of the countries which use a consistent system of P.R. In the first case there develops a multiple system of *related* parties. Half a dozen or more candidates may present themselves in the first ballot, but two major alliances will be formed for the second. In the France of the Third Republic, this tendency was strong enough to limit, as a rule, the second ballot to the contest between the candidates of a united

Right and a united Left. As long as this was the case, there was bound to be a considerable degree of unity both in regard to "men" and in regard to "measures." Actually, the "two blocs" in which political parties were grouped at this time resembled in some of their aspects a system of two parties. Professor René Capitant considered it possible that a two-party system would develop eventually.[35] Few writers went that far, but all agreed with André Siegfried that the division into Right and Left was more significant than the division into political parties inside these groups.

This means, at the same time, that France might, in spite of the second ballot, have progressed toward a parliamentary system with a plebiscitary basis had an effective right of dissolution existed. It is interesting that when, in 1934, Gaston Doumergue tried to free the right of dissolution from some of its fetters, Léon Blum opposed this for the reason that it would imply the grouping of both the Right and Left around one particular leader; the voters, rather than parliament, would make the final choice between these two men. Blum feared that the leader of the Left would always be a Radical, such as Herriot, to whom he would have to play second fiddle. However, as one of his fellow Socialists, Professor Robert, was to point out later, in a very lucid article, Léon Blum himself would, after the election of 1936, have been the leader of the Left with every chance of leading a forceful government. This assumes that he could have wielded the right of dissolution against those elements of his own majority which tended to break away from him. The Senate could not easily have resisted the demands of a Chamber majority based on a direct popular mandate. The title of Robert's article is as significant as are its contents: "An Urgent Innovation: Create the Parliamentary System."[36] It was, in France, indeed necessary to *create* a parliamentary system; what existed under that name both during the Third and the Fourth Republics was something quite different: a government by assembly. The Palais Bourbon, in which the Chamber of Deputies (later the National Assembly) met, was a building without windows, and none could be provided because it was a national monument which had to remain unaltered. As a result, the Chamber was at times referred to as "A House without Windows" in a political sense: The deputies preferred to live a life of

their own, without permitting any clearcut currents of popular senti-
ment to affect their deliberations.

THE EXPLANATION: THE FOURTH REPUBLIC

The leaders of the Resistance were convinced that the defective
institutions of the Third Republic had played their part in the general
disintegration which had preceded the French military collapse in 1940.
The problem was how to bring about a change. During the Third
Republic the vested interests had managed to block all serious attempts
at reform.[37] In 1945 it seemed likely that, if the institutions of the
pre-war period were simply revived, this experience would be repeated.

One way of solving the problem was to draw up a new constitution
before new elections took place. The Resistance Council commissioned
the "General Committee of Studies" (French abbreviation CGE) to
undertake this task. The work was directed by a young man, then
unknown, by the name of Michel Debré, who consulted with as many
others as conditions permitted.[38] When the document[39] was completed
it was sent on to Algiers in the hope that de Gaulle's provisional government would take it as the basis of a definitive project.

The question was how such a competely new political constitution
could be adopted. General de Gaulle could have submitted it to a
plebiscite as he did with the constitution of 1958, or he might simply
have tried to make the project the focus of the discussion, placing his
authority behind its major ideas. His prestige might have succeeded in
breaking down the resistance which the combination of vested interests
and of intellectual confusion was certain to offer.

Actually, discussions hardly reached this point. As soon as the
Communists learned of the draft, they vetoed it, using arguments certain to appeal to those republicans who could not conceive of democracy other than as a "government by assembly." The power of the
Communists was so great because, being able to adapt themselves
easily to the conditions of underground existence, they played a large
part in the Resistance. Also, Roosevelt and Churchill, disturbed by
what they considered a tendency of General de Gaulle toward one-man
rule, forced him to establish close relationship to the political parties
in France, unaware that this amounted to giving the Communists a

veto power on any plans for a new constitution. The Communist pre-
scription for political organization was absolute power for the executive where they expected to control it, but a weak executive, based upon
a combination of "government by assembly" and P.R., wherever they
did not expect to prevail.

Debré's constitution would have blocked such intentions. It is,
however, interesting to note that he rejected not only a "government
by assembly" but also a presidential system on the American model.
The latter, he stated in the Introduction, was not "adapted to the conditions and the political traditions of France." The remedy was to be
found within "the classical form of parliamentary government." This
meant that the President of the Republic had an unlimited right of
parliamentary dissolution, and also that the plurality system of voting
(in multiple-member constituencies) was prescribed in a separate
"organic act." The powers of government were to be concentrated in
the hands of the prime minister but the functions of the President of
the Republic were to be enhanced; he was to be chosen by an enlarged
electoral college not dissimilar to the one prescribed by the constitution
of 1958. The rights of the Chamber of Deputies and of the Senate
were to be limited and those of the government to be extended.

Eventually, the task of writing a new constitution came to be
entrusted to a body in which the vested interests were worse than they
had been in the old Chamber of Deputies and Senate: to a Constituent
Assembly elected under P.R. This meant that the last safeguards were
eliminated which even a weak form of majority voting had provided
during the Third Republic. There was no longer a multiplicity of related, but one of *unrelated* parties. The need to unite, at least in
the second ballot, on one candidate had disappeared; every party could
enter the campaign with its own list, its own dogmas and its own slo-
gans. Each of them was, indeed, proud of its "new freedom," hardly realizing that this meant an unlimited freedom of dissent and disruption.

In addition, P.R. eliminated the pressure under which majority
voting had kept the extremists. During the Third Republic the Communists usually obtained about one-fifth of the seats which P.R. would
have given them (assuming that their popular vote would have been
the same under P.R. as it was under majority voting). In the "popular

front" elections of 1936 they secured (thanks to the mutual support arranged with the other parties of the Left) 72 seats instead of the 93 which P.R. would have given them, yet the effects of the majority system were strong enough to give the moderate Left a majority without the Communist votes which, therefore, could be ignored.

Under P.R. the Communists could translate all the votes which they obtained into seats. They could also expand their popular vote for two reasons: First, votes cast for them were no longer in danger of being "thrown away," and, second, when the Socialists had to cooperate with parties far to their Right, many of their supporters turned to the Communists. It is interesting to note that, when, in September 1945, elections took place for the "general councils," the parliamentary bodies of the *départements* (the so-called "cantonal elections") the Communists, at best, came close to the number of votes obtained by their Socialist rivals,[40] and the latter outscored them more than two to one in regard to seats obtained. Not unnaturally the French Socialists expected to win a victory in the national elections comparable to that obtained by the British Labour party earlier that year; Léon Blum wrote: "We have the wind in the sails." He did not realize to what extent his party's ascendancy over the Communists was due to majority voting. When the first Constituent Assembly was elected under P.R., the Communists immediately outscored the Socialists in terms of votes as well as of seats; eventually, Communist strength came close to being double that of their rivals.

At any rate the basic characteristic of the Constituent Assembly (both the one elected in 1945 and the one elected in 1946) was political pluralism, and the constitution which such a body will write is not a constitution at all. The parties will not establish organs of government capable of acting effectively on behalf of the whole; such organs would have to be controlled by one particular group, and this none of the others would permit. The result has often been compared to medieval feudalism in which each vassal tried to obtain as much power as possible for himself with all of them having a common interest in limiting the power of the center.

A weakening of the executive was, indeed, the major characteristic of the "constitution" of 1946. Specific provisions reduced the competence of both the President of the Republic and of the prime minister. Thus the president could no longer appoint the prime minister and the cabinet directly. He could only "designate" a candidate, who had then to be "invested" by an absolute majority of the National Assembly.

This requirement did make it more difficult to solve a ministerial crisis. Still, the president retained an effective choice among the candidates to be nominated; there was hardly ever a case in which someone could claim to be the effective leader of a majority.

So far as the prime minister and the cabinet are concerned the framers of the 1946 constitution claimed to have eliminated the major sources from which instability had sprung in the past. It was said that a prime minister "endorsed" by an absolute majority of the National Assembly would have a strong position. A vote of confidence (the rejection of which had been the occasion of most crises in the past) could be requested only by the prime minister upon the authorization of the cabinet; there had to be a clear day between the request and the vote. By the same token, a vote of censure necessitated the resignation of a cabinet only if adopted by an absolute majority.

All these provisions did was to provide for the *appearance* of a will to stability where there was none in reality. If there was any doubt as to the true intentions of the framers of the 1946 constitution in regard to executive stability the provisions concerning the right of dissolution would have settled it. The National Assembly could not be dissolved for the first 18 months of its existence. Thereafter, it was necessary for two cabinets to be defeated within an 18-month period with an absolute majority. If this happened, the council of ministers could decree a dissolution which the president had to promulgate. In the original constitution it was also provided that after a dissolution the prime minister was replaced by the president (speaker) of the Assembly, who then appointed a new Minister of the Interior and added to the cabinet "ministers of state" representing parties not in the cabinet; this would have included the Communists. Under these conditions the right of dissolution was, indeed, what Pierre Cot, the brilliant former Radical leader and by then pro-Communist "Progressive," termed, "a wooden sword."

ATTEMPTS AT REFORM

These provisions, and their effects, caused misgivings from the outset. The voters had, on May 5, 1946, rejected the first constitution because it seemed to go altogether too far in the direction of "government by assembly." Only a bare majority of those voting accepted the (slightly changed) second draft; its numbers were inferior to those who had voted for the first version which had been rejected. The M.R.P. had given its — crucial — support to the second constitution only with the understanding that it would soon be revised.[41] Efforts to bring about a reform were incessant, but led only to the minor changes contained in the law of December 7, 1954. Thereafter a designated prime minister would present himself to the National Assembly with his cabinet already chosen; his confirmation required only a simple majority. If this provision made the formation of a new cabinet a little easier it did nothing to make it more stable. Characteristically, there was no change in the requirement of an absolute majority for the adoption of a vote of censure or the rejection of a vote of confidence. To make such a change would have made it easier for a government to proceed to a dissolution — which the members of the Assembly were most anxious to avoid.

The law of December 7, 1954, contained other changes. Thus, a vote on a motion of confidence or of censure could be taken 24 hours after its introduction, without there being a need for a clear day to intervene; the government could adjourn parliament after it had been in session for seven months, and the powers of the Council of the Republic, the weak substitute for the old Senate, were somewhat increased. By and large these changes only proved that there was no desire for a real change. The Fourth Republic seemed as firmly cast in a mold of *immobilisme* as the Third.

Attempts to bring about a reform before there would be a revolution continued nevertheless. Numerous proposals were made[42] and all kinds of compromises were considered. Various "round tables" were organized in order to solve the deadlock on the major reform proposals — but the result was "a dialogue of the deaf." No serious headway was made in the case of the two reforms which mattered: the right of dissolution was not simplified and there was no return to majority voting. Neither change could, of course, be truly effective unless joined to the other. As was demonstrated by the elections of 1956 a dissolution made little sense with P.R. as that system excluded clear alternatives and this did not give the voters a chance to make a genuine political decision. By the same token the experience of the Third Republic made it obvious that majority voting alone (in particular, in the weak version resulting from a second ballot) could not guarantee political stability. The voters could and did provide a relatively homogeneous majority but, as long as the leaders of that majority were unable to renew their contact with the people by resorting, if necessary, to a dissolution, their parliamentary followers felt free to start intriguing against them as soon as they assumed power.

Last-minute attempts to save the Fourth Republic were, however, made when the National Assembly voted, on March 22, 1958, and, more comprehensively, on May 27, 1958, for certain constitutional changes. Only one of them, the denial to the deputies of the right to initiate expenditures, might have been fairly effective; even in this case it must not be overlooked that an omnipotent parliament has ways to bring pressure on a weak government and to make it do its bidding.[43] The government was further to be strengthened by adopting a modified equivalent of the "positive vote of censure" contained in the Bonn constitution, and by giving it a chance (as now provided in Art. 49, Par. 3 of the new constitution) to demand the passage of a proposed measure with the modification that it be considered carried unless a motion of censure was submitted and adopted with an absolute majority.

These provisions look impressive, but what has to be said in regard to them has been summarized in a few words by Jacques Fauvet, one of the editors of *Le Monde*:[44] "The adopted project . . . has the goal to create a majority for the government where there is no majority in parliament." In other words: An attempt was made to square the circle. Under the parliamentary system, in the words of Sir Ivor Jennings:[45] "The effective power of a Government depends essentially on its majority. If it has no majority it may maintain itself in power for a short time by maneuver or intrigue, but it is doomed as soon as the rest of the House combines against it." In England, of course, a majority combining against a government can be expected to be homogeneous, and to be able to form an alternative cabinet. This was not the case in France, where the Communists would always constitute a part of a hostile majority, as would substantial elements of the Right. It was natural enough to make every attempt to thwart such a negative majority. But, then, a government needs a *positive* majority for the enactment of its measures, and it is difficult to see how, under a parliamentary system, it could survive without it.

This question arises also in regard to the argument, advanced so frequently, that only a few of the prime ministers of the Fourth Republic were actually forced to resign by the provisions of the constitution. As a rule, a cabinet was not defeated by an absolute majority. Most prime ministers either yielded to a simple majority or they resigned before there was a vote, knowing that the defection of a part of their supporters made defeat certain. They could have done little else. The precedent for such resignations was set by de Gaulle himself. Under the terms of the provisional constitutional law of November 2, 1945, the Constituent Assembly could not overthrow him once it had elected him. Still, by the end of December 1945 an impasse had been reached in regard to military appropriations. The General declared before the Assembly: "Either you will vote the declaration because you have confidence in the government, or else you will refuse to do so and the government will immediately draw the consequences of this decision."[46] This meant that the government would resign. Shortly afterwards the General did resign without there having been a vote. He just "had enough"; not controlling a majority favorable to his policies he felt impotent. Whatever constitutional law might stipulate, if this happened to the man who had just led a successful struggle for his country's liberation, it is difficult to see how ordinary mortals could have done better.

There was a reason, then, to assume that it was, in certain fields, all but impossible to conduct a constructive policy under the institutional setup of the Fourth Republic, and that the prospects for reforming it by peaceful means were remote. Prime minister after prime minister tried to do the best possible job with the tools at hand. Two of them, Antoine Pinay in 1952 and Pierre Mendés-France in 1954, wielded a considerable authority for a while and developed a genuine popularity in the country. For this very reason they were, however, unpopular with the National Assembly. The deputies not only used the first possible pretext for getting rid of them but also made it clear that they did not want them to return.

This does not mean that nothing was ever accomplished. Actually, even the worst feature of French government, the frequent reversal of governments, had its redeeming aspects. There developed a "Crisis System"[47]: After the resignation of a cabinet political issues were thought through anew and seen in a somewhat larger perspective. Essential measures which had been refused to a particular cabinet might, no matter how haltingly and how grudgingly, be granted to its successor. Thus, Guy Mollet fell over a request for new taxes which were voted to his successor, Maurice Bourgès-Maunoury. The latter fell over the Algerian reform law which was then granted to Félix Gaillard. Gaillard was overthrown because he accepted an Anglo-American "good offices mission" which intended to find a solution for French difficulties with Tunisia. When de Gaulle became Prime Minister he lost little time in making the very type of settlement with Tunisia that had been proposed; in this case had any one of the leaders of the Fourth Republic tried the same policy he would have been swept away by a revolution.

Where there exist so many negative elements and so few positive ones people will still react according to their temperaments. Some will be determined to make the best of a bad situation, working hard to achieve what can be achieved with the means at hand and bending every effort to bring about a peaceful reform. At times there seeemed to be a chance of success as when, in November 1955, the National Assembly first seemed ready, or almost ready, to yield to the popular demand for majority voting. There followed, however, the overthrow of Edgar Faure which necessitated the election of the new National Assembly under the old law. The outcome made, on account of the large Communist strength in the assembly, an electoral reform more difficult than ever. It need not be repeated that while such a step would not have sufficed by itself all the other changes proposed would have meant little without it. It was quite logical when the constitutional reform project voted, late in the day, by the National Assembly on March 21, 1958, ended with the provision that it would not go into effect until a new election law had been adopted.

At any rate, an increasing number of observers reached the conclusion that peaceful reform was impossible; they felt that what was about to fall had best be given a push. This was to be done, in the first place, by what the French call *la politique du pire,*—"the policy of the greater evil." The functioning of the Fourth Republic was not to be facilitated, but to be blocked. Thus, Jacques Soustelle led the assault against the cabinets of Bourgès-Maunoury and Gaillard although he could succeed only because of Communist support. It is interesting to note that even the conservative daily, *Le Figaro,* expressed misgivings in regard to such tactics.[48] On the other hand, Michel Debré[49] left no doubt that only something approaching a national catastrophe, which would lead to the return of General de Gaulle, could bring about a real reform. His friend, Maxime Blocq-Mascart[50] saw in all the discussions of constitutional reform then taking place, such as "round tables" and "free tribunes" in the newspapers, but "different ways of promoting intellectual confusion."

THE REVOLT

The "policy of the greater evil" pursued within the National Assembly was supplemented by preparation for the open use of force. Two fundamental changes in the French political atmosphere made this possible. First, the French Army ceased to be a non-political instrument for the carrying out of national policy, as was pointed out in detail by the military correspondent of the daily, *Le Monde,* Jean Planchais, in a much discussed book published early in 1958.[51] The army smarted under the fact that it had been at war, with brief interruptions, since September 1939, suffering constant losses, in particular among the professional officers, and never achieving a victory for which it could have taken credit — the defeat of the Germans in 1944 and 1945 being due more to Allied than to French efforts.

The war in Indo-China was a turning point. The younger officers felt that they were being "betrayed" not only by the politicians in Paris but also by some of their generals who did the politicians' bidding, whether it made military sense or not. At the same time, it seemed modern war could be won only by adopting some of the methods of "psychological warfare" which Mao-Tse-Tung had taught in China and which Ho Chi-Minh had applied so successfully in Vietnam. The use of such methods was difficult in the framework of a democracy, and more and more officers came to look with disdain not only upon the perversion of democracy which occurred under the Fourth Republic but also upon the very principle of a system in which the government can always be freely criticized by the opposition. The development of this mentality, and the acts which followed from it, were, however, possible only against the background of a political vacuum. As Maurice Duverger[52] put it a few months before the Algerian uprising:

> In the face of a government which governs, of a true government which gives orders, the army will not stir. The playing with disobedience (*les vèlléités de désobéissance*) which manifests itself in certain echelons explains itself by the absence of authority at the top. The army, founded, by its very nature, on command and discipline, is a body without a brain if it no longer receives impulsion from the top. Then its movements become disorderly and accidents are to be feared.

When Duverger wrote these lines he expected that the army could be brought into line with the means available to the Fourth Republic, an expectation held by many at that time, but soon to be refuted by events.

The civilian element was as vital for the "Revolution of May 13"[53] as was the military. There were, first of all, the remnants of the RPF, gathered, for the most part, in the "Social Republican" party. De Gaulle himself was not willing to take the lead in any act of force. He had, however, reached the conclusion that "regimes never reform themselves; they disintegrate and collapse."[54] He was so thoroughly disillusioned with the Fourth Republic that he had "no charitable thought of helping the sick political system to perpetuate itself."[55] His followers acted on the assumption that he would be available as soon as his intervention might appear necessary to save his country from disaster. At any rate, the more ardent Gaullists were determined not to miss any opportunity to change the political image of France.

As C. L. Sulzberger reported two months before the "Algerian revolution": "The last time de Gaulle threatened to come out of retirement and seize the helm in France one of his supporters complained: 'He marched us to the Rubicon; and then he told us to take our fishing rods.' If there is another movement to the Rubicon, there will be no angling party."[56]

What those in France willing to take revolutionary action against the Fourth Republic could do, even with the help of the army and of the white population of Algeria, was limited; de Gaulle's statement of May 15, proclaiming the failure of the "regime of the parties" and his willingness to "assume the powers of the Republic" was of decisive importance. The General added to the impact of his declaration in a press conference, held on May 19,[57] in which he, once again, demonstrated not only a personal force not rivalled by any of the men of the Fourth Republic, but also a mastery of expression which was bound to win him the respect of his opponents. He did not ignore that he was moving at the margin of legality, but he felt that in extreme situations "legitimacy" had to take precedence over "legality" and that the government of the Fourth Republic had long since forfeited any claim to "legitimacy." The General's views were, in fact, shared by some of the outstanding men of the Fourth Republic, who felt that, quite apart from the impossibility of an effective defense against the military threat, there was little that was worth defending, anyway. This is one of the reasons why not only President René Coty, but also Socialists like former President Vincent Auriol and Guy Mollet were willing to ease de Gaulle's way to power; they were, of course, in part motivated by a desire to provide the General with a type of collaboration which would minimize the influence of those of his friends who were not averse to dictatorship.

The question has nevertheless been raised, and will be raised as long as these events are discussed, whether the last governments of the Fourth Republic could not have done more to assert their authority. The answer will have to take into account the general atmosphere of the spring of 1958. In March C. L. Sulzberger,[58] in an article quoted above, stated that "the Gaillard government is not corrupted by power. It is corrupted by the lack of it." A few weeks later, between the middle of April and the middle of May, Gaillard headed a mere caretaker government, characterized by "a serious paralysis of public affairs."[59] At the time of his resignation an American correspondent[60] wrote: "His five months in office left him haggard, looking far older than his 38 years." If, then, he and the men under him bungled during the following weeks there were reasons for it. His successor, Pierre Pflimlin, made a sincere effort to assert his authority against the leaders of the Algerian revolt, although he did not really believe in success. It is hardly relevant whether he and some of his colleagues missed certain opportunities.

At any rate, after May 13 there did exist a serious threat of military insurrection. When Jules Moch, the Socialist Minister of Interior, known for the courage and determination which he had displayed on earlier occasions, surveyed the means of action available to him, he discovered that he could rely neither on the army nor on the police. Open resistance by the government might merely have cleared the path for a military dictatorship, even without a serious civil war. Certainly, there was no real determination in the efforts of the Left to organize the "defense of the Republic," as even the Communists were "somewhat frightened and half-hearted."[61] Nor must we overlook that General de Gaulle enjoyed the goodwill of many members of "left-of-center" groups. As mentioned above, Hubert Beuve-Méry, the publisher of *Le Monde,* had expressed himself in terms calculated to promote the General's acceptance by wavering republicans. Professor Maurice Duverger (who was, however, to oppose the new constitution) published, in early March, an article under the title "Quand?"[62] The "When?" referred to the time of the General's return to power; the event itself was considered inevitable.

When the final crisis of the Fourth Republic began with the resignation of Premier Gaillard on April 15, de Gaulle was as anxious to adhere to the legal forms of the existing constitution as he was determined not to become a "prisoner of the system." He wanted to avoid what happened in 1945 and 1946, when the framing of the country's new institutions came to be controlled by the vested interests. Therefore, he insisted that the National Assembly not only accept him and his cabinet, as was done by a vote of 329 to 224 on June 1, but that he also be free from parliamentary pressure during a period of transition. This was accomplished by the act of June 2 which gave him plenary powers for a six-month period by a vote of 322 to 232. Finally, the procedure to be followed in the revision of the constitution of 1946 was to be modified. Art. 90 required a two-thirds majority of the National Assembly (or else a three-fifths majority by both the Assembly and the Council of the Republic), if a referendum, which would have meant a substantial delay, was to be avoided. The General threatened to resign unless he received the majority, which would set Art. 90 aside and make it possible for him to have a new constitution drawn up which would be submitted to the people in a referendum; on June 2 this request was granted by a vote of 350 to 161.[63] Both the grant of plenary powers, and the right to draw up the new constitution, were subject to reservations intended to guarantee the respect for the essential principles of republican government. De Gaulle showed himself conciliatory in the discussion of all details. As a deputy put it, "operation sedition" (the "revolution" of May 13) was followed by "operation seduction," the winning over, by persuasion, of a large parliamentary majority.

The drafting of the new constitution was entrusted to a committee headed by Senator Michel Debré, the new Minister of Justice. A few months earlier, he had defined in detail the procedure which was to govern the transition from the Fourth Republic to the Fifth;[64] his plans were to be followed closely. The cabinet approved the draft of the new constitution on July 26, and on July 29 there began the meetings of the "Consultative Constitutional Committee" which consisted of 26 members of parliament (but no Communists) and 19 experts; Paul Reynaud was elected as its chairman. Its task was purely advisory, but it did submit a detailed report which was to lead to certain changes in the original draft[65] which was also examined by the Council of State. There were, finally, extensive criticisms by experts in the field[66] whose views failed, however, either to bring about important modifications, or even to impress the public.

THE NEW CONSTITUTION

THE PRESIDENT

THE FIRST DECISION OF THE constitution-makers was whether they should limit themselves to establishing in France a "genuine" parliamentary system, based on majority voting and an untrammelled right of dissolution, or whether they wanted to go in the direction of a presidential system similar to that of the United States. In the past the leading Gaullist experts had preferred the first alternative. Debré did so when he drew up the reform plan of the "General Committee of Studies" and René Capitant[67] had, on an earlier occasion, warned against any "dualism" which the conferring of independent powers upon the president would entail. By 1958 conditions had, however, become very different from what they had been during the Third Republic. During the latter's final period René Capitant[68] could write: ". . . we have sixteen or seventeen parliamentary groups, but . . . [as] André Siegfried . . . has shown and explained so admirably: in the elections there are only two parties, the Right and the Left. . . . Two parties, but that is exactly the condition of parliamentarism!" By 1958 what had been a potentially adequate basis for creating a genuine parliamentary system had disappeared. A government with the required degree of cohesion could not be expected to develop simply from combining a return to majority voting with an effective right of parliamentary dissolution. Michel Debré considered it necessary to take more direct measures calculated to bring about a strengthening of the executive.[69]

General de Gaulle had never been favorable to the parliamentary system, and he had demanded steps to create a real executive ever since he delivered his famous speech in Bayeux[69a] in 1946. For him, the executive consisted, however, not primarily of the prime minister[70] and the cabinet, but also, and above all, of the head of the state. As a result the new constitution does indeed go far toward emphasizing the powers of the president. Its predecessor had mentioned the chief of state only in its Title VI, beginning with Art. 93, as the very last of the organs of the government. The new document deals with the president in Title II, beginning with Article 5, before either parliament or the cabinet are mentioned. The president's new status begins with the mode of his election. He is no longer chosen by a parliamentary assembly, but by an electoral college of almost 80,000 members, consisting for the most part of local officials and of members and delegates of municipal councils of the larger cities.

It would, of course, have been more logical to have the president elected by direct popular vote. In republican France this procedure was, after its abuse by the two Napoleons, still regarded as a hallmark of dictatorship. A direct popular vote would, however, have avoided the involuntary gerrymandering of the present system, which is weighed in favor of the small, and mostly rural, municipalities.[71] Yet it is difficult to see how the president can be a power in his own right unless he is the choice of a true majority. In the case of General de Gaulle there was no problem but future presidents would be clearly at a disadvantage if they should owe their election to a minority segment of the population.

So far as the concrete powers of the president are concerned, the constitution confers upon him both the rights normally held by the head of the state under a parliamentary system, and others which are inspired by the presidential system. Thus, the president appoints the prime minister and, on his recommendation, the members of the cabinet (Art. 8). He terminates the functions of the prime minister when the latter presents to him the resignation of his government. He further presides over the council of ministers (Art. 9), as was the custom both during the Third and the Fourth Republics. He promulgates laws, although he can demand a new deliberation on measures which he opposes (Art. 10). He may, on the proposal of the government, submit laws dealing with the structure of the government, or entailing the approval of treaties, or a change in the relationships with the members of the French community (which comprises France and the former colonies) to a referendum (Art. 11). He may further dissolve the National Assembly, although once it has been dissolved he cannot do so again until a year after the new elections (Art. 12). The president has far-reaching powers of appointment (Art. 13). He accredits and receives ambassadors (Art. 14); he is chief of the armed forces (Art. 15). He has the right of pardon (Art 18), and he communicates with parliament by way of special messages (Art. 18). Extended powers are conferred upon him in the field of foreign affairs. Art. 52 reads:

> The President of the Republic shall negotiate and ratify treaties.
> He shall be informed of all negotiations leading to the conclusion of an international agreement not subject to ratification.

On the other hand, according to Art. 53, the more important treaties may be "ratified and approved only by a law."

Some of these powers clearly exceed what is customary under the parliamentary system. They might, however, all be more or less nullified through the requirement of countersignature by a responsible minister. The head of the state is not responsible for his act (except by impeachment, which is hardly practical) whereas the prime minister and the cabinet are. In a democratic state responsibility and power go together. It would not make sense to ask a cabinet to assume responsibility for measures of which it does not approve, nor would it be logical to let the head of the state make far-reaching decisions for which he would not be answerable. Wherever the requirement of countersignature applies, it cuts the Gordian knot: All of the rights entrusted legally to the president are in reality exercised by the prime minister and the cabinet. The exceptions lie in those areas where a system based on the alternation of political parties cannot function, such as in the selection of a new prime minister when there is more than one candidate who can hope to secure a parliamentary majority. Also, the head of the state may always exercise "influence" where he has no direct "power"; this may be facilitated by provisions of the constitution which require his explicit approval for certain measures.

The Constitution of the Fifth Republic explicitly exempts important acts of the president from the requirement of countersignature (Art. 19). These are: The appointment of the prime minister, the demand for a referendum, the dissolution of the National Assembly, the proclamation of a state of emergency, messages to parliament, referring matters to the Constitutional Council, and the appointment of one-third of the members of the Constitutional Council. The president's powers in regard to treaties are subject to the requirement of countersignature, although *The Economist*[72] commented: "The provision of the new French constitution — that 'the President negotiates treaties' — must be interpreted as meaning that he effectively runs the country's foreign policy."

If there were any doubt on the subject, the constitutional intent to make the president into a power of his own is clearly conveyed by Art. 5, which reads:

> The President of the Republic shall see that the Constitution is respected. He shall ensure, by his arbitration, the regular functioning of the governmental authorities, as well as the continuance of the state.
>
> He shall be the guarantor of national independence, of the integrity of the territory, and of respect for Community agreements and treaties.

The powers which these words contemplate are clearly intended to go far beyond the ones normally accorded to the President of the Republic. On the other hand, essential features of the parliamentary system are retained. The members of the cabinet are not, as in the United States, mere presidential assistants, subjected to his orders. Art. 20 says that "The Government shall determine and direct the policy of the nation." In addition, according to Art. 21, "The premier shall direct the operation of the government." At the same time Arts. 49 and 50 stipulate that the government is responsible to the National Assembly (even if this responsibility is surrounded by provisions intended to make the overthrow of a cabinet as difficult as possible), and that it has to resign if either a vote of censure has been adopted or if "the National Assembly disapproves the program or a declaration of general policy of the government."

In its major outlines, then, parliamentary government is to be retained. Clearly, when the president selects the prime minister he must choose someone likely to be approved by a majority. In theory a new government need not go before parliament and ask for a vote of confidence, but in fact it is logical to do so. At any rate, when the Debré cabinet was formed it did present itself to the National Assembly and thereby set a precedent which is likely to be followed in the future. The cabinet, then, stands between two centers of power: parliament (in particular the National Assembly) and the president. The question is which of the two will, in the long run, constitute the center of gravity. Certainly, if a president should insist on a political direction different from that of a majority of the National Assembly there would be a dualism laden with conflict.

This is one of the problems which is obscured by the concrete situation which prevailed when the new constitution was put into effect. Not only did the referendum on the constitution leave no doubt that the voters wanted a Gaullist policy adopted, but the results of the Assembly elections of November 23 and 30 must be interpreted in the same way. The strong majority of the Union for the New Republic (U.N.R.) and the Independents was unexpected. It was not what de Gaulle desired, but it was what the people *thought* he desired. The deputies could not ignore these wishes, in particular since, if they had acted contrary to a clear popular mandate, de Gaulle could have dissolved the Assembly. Furthermore, since majority voting had been restored, the U.N.R. and the Independents, in particular the former, were likely to lose numerous seats which had been won by a small margin. This time the leaders would have been exposed to almost as great a risk as the rank and file of their followers; under P.R., with the top men of a party heading its tickets, the situation had been different.

De Gaulle, at any rate, took steps to strengthen the position of the presidential office. He did not, as his predecessors had done, limit himself to a small group of men whose primary function was to maintain liaison with the government. Instead, he set up elaborate services of his own, soon taxing the capacity of the Elysée, the presidential palace, and giving rise to the rumor that his office was to be transferred to more spacious quarters outside Paris.

Nor did he leave any doubt as to the fact that he intended to use the powers conferred upon him by the constitution. In the address delivered on the occasion of his inauguration[73] he declared that it was his duty to represent the common interests of the nation and the community and even to "impose" them, since "these are my obligations." He added: "In this I shall not fail—I bear witness to that in advance." He elucidated this interpretation of his functions by holding, on March 27, a press conference in the Elysée,[74] something which no president of the Third or Fourth Republic had done. In regard to his budgetary and economic measures, which had encountered much criticism, he added that they had been taken in consequence of the powers conferred upon the government by the referendum of September 28, and that this popular mandate could be modified only by "a referendum or by new elections." In other words, the National Assembly was put on notice that it would be dissolved if it proved unwilling to support the president's policies.

De Gaulle could take such a stand on account of his great popularity, but the actual significance of the presidency as an institution remains for the future to decide. Some hold that the General has established a trend which will lead to an executive of the American type. Others expect a development in the direction of a parliamentary system with a stronger government than existed under the Third and Fourth Republic. Others again are afraid of a dictatorship, not only on account of the fact that the turbulent forces which brought de Gaulle to power remained a factor, but also because certain provisions of the constitution would, in their opinion, facilitate such a course.

This applies, in particular, to Art. 16 of the new constitution, easily its most controversial part. It states that, when the institution of the republic, or the country's independence, "are threatened in a grave and immediate manner" and when, at the same time "the regular functioning of the constitutional government authorities is interrupted" the president may (without countersignature) after consultation with the premier, the presidents of the parliamentary assemblies and the Constitutional Council, take whatever measures he deems necessary. The measures must be prompted by the desire to ensure to the constitutional governmental authorities, in the shortest possible time, the means of fulfilling their assigned function. At the same time, "Parliament shall meet by right"; the National Assembly may not be dissolved during such period.

These conditions are, indeed, sweeping, and Maurice Duverger[75] has spoken of "the terrible Article 16." On the other hand, critics have been reminded that what General de Gaulle had in mind was the type of situation which developed in June 1940, when everything collapsed and when, in his opinion, a president endowed with such powers might have rallied the nation. More recently, his supporters, including Michel Debré,[76] have referred to the possibility of a nuclear war. Reference might also be made to the general trend to make allowance for the need of a "Crisis Government"[77] adequate to whatever emergency may arise.

It is, however, well to bear in mind that where a parliamentary system functions on the basis of a two-party system, such as in England, there is no need for emergency powers. In that case a government can, as long as it is in firm control of a parliamentary majority, do what it considers necessary; if it should have to deviate from existing laws it could count on a bill of indemnity. For France it might again be argued that as long as no clearcut majorities exist, special rules are needed. Logically such powers would belong, however, to the government rather than to the president; they might formally have been entrusted to the latter but with the understanding that the requirement of countersignature — specifically excluded in regard to Art. 16 — would place their exercise into the hands of the cabinet, even if this is one of the cases in which the advice tendered by the head of the state could be expected to carry considerable weight.

Clearly, the way in which General de Gaulle has exercised his functions has satisfied most observers that he would not abuse his emergency powers. But, it is asked,[78] what might a different president do, in particular, one bent as much on forcing on the country a policy of his own as Alexandre Millerand was in 1924. In such a case units of the army might agree to provide him with an appearance of an emergency. He would, of course, act contrary to the spirit of Art. 16, according to which the use of the emergency powers must have no purpose other than to render a normal functioning of the government possible. An abuse might, however, not be easy to check; therefore the "Consultative Constitutional Committee" had suggested that the "Constitutional Council," rather than the president, decide whether an emergency existed.

Actually, whatever use is made of Art. 16 depends on the general climate of the country. If this climate is even as favorable to democracy as it was under the Third Republic an abuse would be difficult. It was said that while the Third Republic governed badly, it defended itself well: Whenever there was an attack upon it, a clear popular majority rallied to its defense and defeated its enemies. In this respect as in others it will take the Fifth Republic time to regain ground lost by the Fourth, but there is at least a chance that this will be done under the combined effect of majority voting and the right of dissolution. As soon as this point is reached, Art. 16 will look less ominous than it now does to some observers.

GOVERNMENT AND PARLIAMENT

Meanwhile, there is the problem whether the provisions concerning the prime minister and the cabinet will exercise an influence of their own. It may prove of some significance that while, according to Art. 8, the president appoints the prime minister outright, he shall "terminate the functions of the premier when the latter presents the resignation of the cabinet." The initiative for a resignation, then, is to come from the prime minister who, presumably, will stay in office as long as he is supported by a majority. This rule had been interpreted to mean that "the government, following the classical parliamentary technique, constitutes an autonomous political force and that it is not entirely submitted to the discretion of the head of the state."[79]

Once again there is a difference between conditions prevailing with a de Gaulle at the peak of his power and those which may be expected to develop at a later time. Prime Minister Debré has never left any doubt that his only intention is to implement the policies determined by his chief; this implies that he would resign if asked to do so. His successors may, however, owe their positions more to the wishes of a parliamentary majority than to the endorsement of a president who is likely to lack the popular prestige of a de Gaulle. They will be able to point to Art. 20 of the constitution which says that "the Government shall determine and direct the policy of the nation. It shall have at its disposal the administration and the armed forces." Furthermore, Art. 21 stipulates that "the Premier shall direct the operation of the government." In the hands of a government supported by a coherent majority these provisions provide ample justification for the claim that the cabinet is entitled to a policy of its own.

The new constitution is based on the assumption that the president and the cabinet will work in harmony; it intends to enhance the position of the executive as a whole as against parliament, but there is no lack of possibilities of conflict. Thus, the right of dissolving the National Assembly is one of those granted the president without the requirement of countersignature (Arts. 12 and 19). Ordinarily, a dissolution is regarded as a means by which a cabinet, when threatened by parliament, can appeal directly to the people, even if it is assumed that the psychological effects of the existence of this right are expected to be more important than its actual exercise. The logic of the system, then, tends to place the weapon of dissolution into the hands of the cabinet, at whose request the head of the state is expected to act even if the right is formally entrusted to him.

Under de Gaulle the function of the right of dissolution was to fortify both the president and the government against possible whims of a somewhat accidental majority. If, however, the right of dissolution should ever become a weapon used by the president against a cabinet and a parliamentary majority acting in harmony with it the result would be a grave constitutional crisis.

CABINET AND PARLIAMENT

Let us now consider those provisions of the constitution which, while stipulating the cabinet's responsibility to the National Assembly, endeavor to safeguard it against crises. Thus, if the National Assembly takes the initiative in challenging the government, it must, according to Art. 49, Par. 2, do so by a formal motion of censure; this must be signed by at least one-tenth of its members. The vote cannot take place until 48 hours have elapsed. Only the votes cast in favor of the motion are counted, and unless they amount to more than half of the Assembly's membership the motion has been defeated.

A similar provision intended to make it impossible to overthrow the government except by an absolute majority of the Assembly's members is contained in Par. 3 of Art. 49: The Prime Minister may, after deliberation in the Council of Ministers (presided over by the President of the Republic) engage the government's responsibility on the vote of a text, which shall be deemed to have been accepted unless a motion of censure, to be introduced during the succeeding 24 hours, is adopted by an absolute majority of the Assembly's members. If the motion is rejected, its signatories may not introduce another in the course of the same session.

It is interesting to note that Art. 49 also implies the possibility that the government can be overthrown by a simple majority of the National Assembly. In the first paragraph it is stated that the Prime Minister may, after deliberation in the Council of Ministers, engage the responsibility of the government to the National Assembly with regard to the program of the government or with regard to a declaration of general policy. No absolute majority is specified; it would seem to follow that the government's request may be refused by a simple majority. Art. 50 states, however, that the government must resign in this case as well as in that of a vote of censure. In other words, whenever the government itself takes the initiative to have the Assembly pass on its program and its policies it must resign if defeated with a simple majority. This is difficult to reconcile with the general tendencies of the constitution but it is, in the opinion of the most competent observers, a fact. If we take into account that the government's request for a vote of confidence has, in the past, been much more frequent than a motion of censure, it is obvious that the elaborate requirement of an absolute majority may, for this reason alone, be ineffective. The procedural attempts to stabilize the government seem, therefore, as artificial as those proposed during the dying days of the Fourth Republic on which they are patterned. The strength displayed by the Debré government was due to the knowledge of the deputies that any defeat of a major government measure would mean a dissolution, in which the prestige of General de Gaulle would be thrown against them.

It must be added that, while Art. 50 speaks of cases in which the government must resign only in connection with the votes by the National Assembly, the Prime Minister may also ask the Senate for the approval of a general policy declaration (Art. 49, Par. 4). Besides, Art. 20 states that the government "shall be responsible to Parliament under the conditions and according to the procedure stipulated in Arts. 49 and 50." The term "parliament" includes the Senate, although there is no explicit requirement that the government must resign when placed in a minority by the Senate. The intention was, apparently, that that body should not be in a position to overthrow the government. However, nothing prevents a cabinet from resigning voluntarily, if it is defeated in the Senate. On the other hand, the fact that the new Senate does not have the absolute veto over legislation enjoyed by the Senate of the Third Republic strengthens the hands of a government supported by a majority of the Assembly. Still, the Senate cannot be dissolved; it may therefore take a more independent attitude towards the government than the National Assembly, even if it cannot prevail and must rely upon wearing a government out rather than defeating it.

Let us now consider the elaborate rules calculated to enhance the powers of the government in regard to parliament. They apply in the first place to parliamentary procedure. During the Third and Fourth Republics the determination of the parliamentary timetables was left entirely to the officials of the two houses, although since 1954 a feeble attempt was made to give the government a voice. Now Art. 48 of the constitution provides that "The discussion of the bills filed or agreed upon by the Government shall have priority on the agenda of the assemblies in the order set by the Government." Also, according to Art. 42, the first of the two chambers to which the government submits a bill must deliberate on the basis of this version; it is, therefore, no longer possible for parliamentary committees to submit a completely changed draft. Furthermore, while, according to Art. 44, members of both the government and of parliament can propose amendments to a bill the government may, after the opening of the debate, oppose the consideration of any amendment not previously submitted in committee. What these provision are to accomplish has been achieved in other countries, notably England, by the rules of parliamentary procedure. The introduction of such rules could not be expected in France, and, therefore, there were reasons to adopt the constitutional provisions in question.

On the other hand the functions of the French parliament do seem to have been interfered with unduly by the limitation of sessions prescribed in Art. 28. There are now two ordinary sessions. The first extends from the first Tuesday of October to the third Friday of December The second begins on the last Tuesday in April and is to last no longer than three months. Extraordinary sessions may be held both at the request of the prime minister or of the majority of the Assembly's members (Art. 29), but in the latter case they cannot extend for more than 12 days. It is generally resented that there can be no regular sessions between January and April, the most active months of the year. The reason given is that during this time the Senate of the Community (as provided in Art. 83 of the constitution) is to meet; most of its members are deputies or senators. One wonders, however, whether the meetings of this body and of the French parliament could not without undue inconvenience have been allowed to overlap. It is interesting to note that the arrangement of parliamentary sessions has been criticized even by Gaullists such as Professor Marcel Prélot.[80]

Among the provisions born out of the distrust of parliament the one most pregnant with difficulties is Art. 23, which stipulates that members of the government may not belong to parliament. The demand for this rule, which incidentally proved quite popular among the voters, was made by non-Gaullists as well as by Gaullists. It was, to some extent, a logical result of the advocacy of the presidential system which developed during the final years of the Fourth Republic; as sincere a republican as François Goguel[81] was among those who asked for a separation of parliamentary and ministerial functions. Since, however, the Constitution of the Fifth Republic aims at a modified parliamentary, rather than a presidential system, the question arises whether the incompatability between parliamentary mandate and membership of the cabinet will serve its purpose. The underlying assumption, formulated vigorously by Maurice Duverger,[82] is that, as long as the deputies can hope that by overthrowing a cabinet they may become ministers themselves, they will overthrow cabinets; they are less likely to do so if, in order to become ministers, they must cease being deputies. Yet, one wonders whether the right of dissolution and the majority system of voting are to be assumed ineffective in regard to the necessary tempering of the parliamentary appetites?

The drawbacks of the new rule are obvious. In Walter Bagehot's[83] words:

> A great popular assembly has a corporate character; it has its own privileges, prejudices, and notions. And one of these notions is that its own members — the persons it sees every day — whose qualities it knows, whose minds it can test, are those whom it can most trust. A clerk speaking from without would be an unfamiliar object. He would be an outsider. He would speak under suspicion; he would speak without dignity. Very often he would speak as a victim.

These remarks pertain primarily to cabinet members taken from outside political life; those who have belonged to a parliamentary body in the past will know better how to handle it. Even they will suffer from the fact that they are no longer the colleagues of those whom they are trying to lead; to some extent they, too, will be looked upon as strangers.

Difficulties are greater for cabinet members taken from the ranks of the bureaucracy, the army, or industrial managers. These men will suffer from all the "limitations of the expert," of which Michel Debré[84] showed a clear awareness in an earlier publication. They have, above all, little knowledge of the psychological factors involved in political decisions. Harry S Truman[85] was right when he said: "A politician is a man who understands people. He's got to understand the country." While democratic leaders should take the long view of their country's interests and be willing to assume risks in order to serve them, they should also know how to make the people see the reasons for their actions. This is an art in which even the best administrative, military or economic expert has no training, even if he should possess the basic aptitude.

French governments, will, of course, always contain men with political experience. Thus, when Michel Debré announced the composition of his cabinet on January 9, 1959,[86] twelve of the ministers were members, or former members, of either the National Assembly or the Senate; nine were not. The latter included the Minister of Foreign Affairs, the Minister of Defense, as well as the Ministers of Education, of Industry and Commerce, and of Construction. These men headed important departments which would have benefitted from having a genuine political leader as their spokesman who could, at the same time, have imparted a dynamic impulse to the civil servants in the ministries. Within a few months after the formation of the cabinet special measures had to be taken in order to establish an effective liaison between it and its majority, as well as between the cabinet and the people; where the members of a government are the active leaders of a parliamentary majority both tasks are taken care of automatically.

The final anomaly of Art. 23 resulted from the desire to provide members of parliament who became ministers with a chance to regain their seats. Every candidate for the Assembly or the Senate must run together with a substitute whose name appears on the ballots. The substitute takes over the seat vacated when its holder becomes a minister, or assumes any government position (except in the case of extraordinary assignments lasting no more than six months), or when he dies. By-elections are abolished in these cases—another feature tending to make the government less sensitive to public opinion than it might be. There are, however, by-elections in certain other cases, particularly when an election is invalidated or when a deputy or senator resigns.[87] Substitutes may not, in the next election, be candidates for seats for which they were nominated; they can, therefore, not become the rivals of those whom they replace. Their situation is, however, equivocal enough to provoke a good measure of irony.[88] At the same time, a minister's chance to regain his seat can be rather remote. A deputy who becomes a minister may have to wait five years before he can return to the Assembly, although for a senator the interval is never longer than three years since any seat filled by a substitute is subject to election whenever a third of the Senate is renewed.

It should be noted in passing, however, that Michel Debré "was not opposed to by-elections for replacing deputies who had resigned after becoming ministers, thinking for a time of permitting them to run for reelection immediately themselves, as in England prior to 1926."[88a] This is one of the cases[89] in which restrictive measures are due to the "Ministers of State" who represented the old political parties in General de Gaulle's cabinet; Guy Mollet, in particular, pointed out that his party was opposed to by-elections.

As long as ministers are not members of parliament the government cannot, of course, rely upon their votes, although the substitutes may consider it their duty to support cabinets to which their associates belong.[90] It is interesting to note that some French observers, including Michel Debré,[91] consider it improper for ministers to vote for themselves; they refer to the early days of the Third Republic when this was not done. An entirely different attitude prevails, however, in England. Thus, Sir Ivor Jennings, [92] refers to the fact that members of the government must, unless they are members of the House of Lords, belong to the House of Commons, and continues:

> This is in itself a factor of great importance. It lies at the root of Cabinet Government as the British Constitution understands it. It is the essential characteristic of the British parliamentary system — though that is to say the same thing in a different way. The ministers and officers of the Royal Household in the House of Commons number some forty. Each minister has an unpaid parliamentary private secretary, bringing the total number of persons with an official or quasi-official position up to about seventy. Where the parties are fairly evenly divided it follows that the Government secures the approval of its proposals only because its members vote for themselves.

There is, in fact, no reason why members of a parliamentary body should not vote for a government to which they belong. When the voters choose a member of the House of Commons they express a preference for a government. If those who belong to this government could not vote for it their electors would be without spokesmen in regard to the most important decisions to be made.

The same logic holds in France, and one wonders whether it will not, in the end, prevail. The intention was to do away with that which Michel Debré called "the race for the portfolios";[93] the deputies and senators were to be subjected to what André Siegfried[94] termed a "cure of reeducation." They needed it, but even the most thorough cure is not intended to last forever. Is it not possible to hope that, once a new leaf has been turned over, France's parliamentarians will no longer succumb to an unbridled and unprincipled desire for ministerial posts?[95] In that case the incompatibility between parliamentary mandate and membership in the government could be ended.

Let us now turn to the distribution of legislative authority between the government and parliament, as set forth in Title V of the constitution (Arts. 34-49). The general rule that "All laws shall be passed by parliament" (Art. 34) is followed by a great many restrictions. There is a detailed list of the matters which are to be dealt with by law; all others shall be deemed to have a "regulative character" (Art. 37) to be ordered by government decree. In addition, the government can ask parliament to permit it for a limited period to enact "ordinances" on matters which are "ordinarily within the domain of the law" (Art. 38). This is the equivalent of the "plenary powers" voted repeatedly during the final decades of the Third Republic, which the Constitution of the Fourth Republic tried in vain to outlaw. If the governments of the Fifth Republic are reasonably strong they will not need such special powers.

This is not the place to discuss further details,[96] nor is it necessary. The actual division of labor between government and parliament will depend less on the written constitution than on the basic power relationships in the country's political life. During the initial period of 1958-60 even after the new constitution had gone into effect, all important decisions were made by General de Gaulle, whether they were in the legislative or the executive fields. Future developments depend on the degree of political power which the president and the prime minister will wield in regard to parliament, and vice versa. A comparatively coherent parliamentary majority, supported by the people, will force the government to let it out of the doghouse and to make it an effective partner, ending some of the numerous and detailed restrictions now imposed upon it. In one case the constitution contemplates such a possibility; the last paragraph of Art. 34 provides that the distinction between the province of laws and that of "ordinances" may be "developed in detail and amplified by an organic law." This is one of the innovations due to the advice of the Council of State; it could serve as a start for establishing a new relationship between government and parliament.

THE SENATE

Now a few words on the new Senate. Its powers lie between those granted to the Senate of the Third Republic which, in constitutional theory, was the equal of the Chamber of Deputies, and those of the Fourth Republic's Council of the Republic, whose rights were minor. The authors of the new constitution wisely resisted the temptation to make the Senate once again the equal of the National Assembly. In that case, legislation accepted by the Senate could be held up indefinitely; also, there might once again have been two bodies able to overthrow the cabinet.

According to Art. 43 both chambers share with the government the right to initiate legislation. In principle, legislation requires the consent of both houses (Art. 45). If, after two readings in both assemblies, no agreement has been reached, or if the government deems the matter urgent after a single reading, the prime minister shall have the right to arrange for the meeting of a joint committee of the two houses, with an equal number of members from both. The government may submit a text approved by this committee to the Assembly and the Senate; no amendment shall be admissable except by permission of the government. If the committee fails to agree on a text, or the two houses fail to accept the proposal of the committee the government may, after a new reading by both houses, ask the National Assembly to make the final decision. The latter is empowered to proceed either from the text prepared by the joint committee, or the last text adopted by itself; it may also accept amendments made by the Senate.

This procedure is simple. Both houses have their say, but if they cannot agree, the government can break the deadlock with the help of the National Assembly. That the initiative should lie in the hands of the government is natural; it is a part of the logic of the parliamentary system. Similar considerations apply to Art. 44, Par. 3, which stipulates that upon request by the government "the Assembly concerned shall decide, by a single vote, on all or part of the text under discussion, retaining only the amendments proposed or accepted by the Government." If this rule is not used to restrict debate unduly, it will be comparable in its effects to the rules of "closure" in the House of Commons.

Special provisions are also made to guarantee a timely adoption of the budget (Art. 47). The government has various means[97] at its disposal to press for its passage. In the end, "Should Parliament fail to reach a decision within a time limit of seventy days, the provisions of the bill may be enforced by ordinance." This, then, makes it impossible for the budget to be held up well into the new fiscal year as happened repeatedly in the past; once again, however, the assumption is made that the parliaments of the Fifth Republic might, in spite of all changes, attempt to follow in the footsteps of their predecessors.

To return to the special problems of the Senate: It has, in the initial stages of law, the same powers as the National Assembly, but can, in the end, be overridden by a decision of the latter body initiated by the government. So far as a vote of censure is concerned, the entire procedure takes place before the National Assembly. The Senate has enough power to perform the functions of a "Chamber of Reflection" but it is not powerful enough to engage in some of the obstructive tactics charged to the Senate of the Third Republic.

The Senate is, of course, an indirectly elected body; its political weight is further reduced by the fact that the representation of the rural areas is disproportionately large. Separate electoral colleges are formed in each *département*. The center of gravity rests with the municipalities of less than 1500 inhabitants. For the Senate of 1959 these small communes, representing 33 per cent of the population chose 53 per cent of the senatorial electors.[98] As a result the new Senate has, like its predecessors under the Third and Fourth Republics, been called a "Chamber of Agriculture." If there is a grain of truth in this charge, it is also true that the Senate is a great deal more than a representative of economic interests. The length of the senatorial term (again nine years as under the Third Republic, whereas it was six years for the Council of the Republic) attracts able men, in particular those who do not feel equal to the arduous campaign required for election to the National Assembly. In 1959 the fact that so many leaders of the Fourth

Republic were defeated in the Assembly elections of 1958 caused the influx of a considerable array of political talent into the first Senate of the Fifth Republic, increasing the prestige of the institution.

MINOR PROVISIONS

There remain several minor provisions concerning the new status of the French parliament. Thus, Art. 40 deprives the deputies and the senators of the possiblity of initiating new expenditures, a matter which, in England, has been settled by a simple standing order for more than two centuries.

A further restriction on parliament results from Art. 59, according to which the Constitutional Council rules on the validity of elections. This is a minor, but useful reform. When past French parliaments ruled on contested elections, partisan considerations were frequently in evidence and valuable time was lost. Thus, when Guy Mollet presented his cabinet to the National Assembly elected in January, 1956, he emphasized the need for speedy action in regard to constitutional and electoral reform. The time which might have been devoted to these subjects was, however, taken up by a prolonged discussion of the right of a number of Poujadist deputies to their seats. The procedure by which eventually 11 Poujadists were deprived of their seats had a good legal basis. Still, it impressed the general public unfavorably, and left tempers disturbed within the National Assembly. The Constitutional Council can handle such matters expeditiously and more impartially.

Finally, Art. 32 provides that the President (speaker) of the National Assembly is elected for the full term of that body, and the President of the Senate every three years after the renewal of one-third of its membership. In the past the election of these officers took place every year in January. Changes were not frequent but, in the National Assembly at least, there always developed an element of uncertainty and of agitation which it was well to eliminate.

THE CONSTITUTIONAL COUNCIL

Another innovation consists in the creation of the Constitutional Council (Arts. 56-63). In addition to the former Presidents of the Republic it consists of nine members whose term of office is nine years (no second term is possible), and one-third of the membership is renewed every year. Three are appointed by the President of the Republic (without countersignature), three by the President of the National Assembly, and three by the President of the Senate. Councillors may not be members of either the cabinet or of parliament.[99]

The Council examines presidential as well as contested parliamentary elections. It has to pass on all constitutional laws ("organic laws"[100], which are intended to supplement constitutional provisions concerning the organs of government, and are enacted under conditions a little more difficult than those applying to ordinary laws). Likewise, the rules of the parliamentary assemblies are submitted to the Council. Finally, laws may before their promulgation be submitted to the Council by the President of the Republic, the Premier, or either of the presidents of the Assembly or the Senate. The Council decides the issue of constitutionality; any measure which it declares unconstitutional may not be promulgated or implemented. Its decision is final and binds all government authorities, including the judiciary.

It was one of the purposes of this new institution to convince critics of the constitution that its provisions would not be interpreted arbitrarily. In addition, there was the influence of the fact that the judicial review of legislative acts has, in recent years, been extended to countries with parliamentary government, such as Germany and Italy. The results have not always been satisfactory. In Italy weak governments have found their position further burdened.[101] In the Federal Republic of Germany governments have, so far, been strong and stable, but the Constitutional Court has introduced additional problems, apart from the uncertainty which hangs over an enactment the constitutionality of which has been, or may be, challenged.[102] The solution adopted in France would, on the whole, seem more satisfactory, in particular since all decisions must be made within a reasonably short time, and before a measure is promulgated. It is interesting to note that the suggestion of the "Consultative Constitutional Committees," according to which one-third of the members of the National Assembly could have challenged the constitutionality of any law, was rejected. Had it been adopted any opposition disposing of a third of the Assembly's membership could have fought the majority with legal weapons after it had lost the political fight. In such cases there is a danger of what Karl Loewenstein[103] called the "judicialization of political dynamics." The French regulation has avoided this and yet established a minimum of constitutional safeguards. While, in the eyes of many, it does not go far enough, it has at least the merit of not creating complications of its own.

So far as the other organs provided for in the constitution are concerned we may disregard the Economic and Social Council (Arts. 69-71). Its functions are purely advisory and the potentialities of such a body are usually overestimated.[104] For similar reasons we need not discuss the provisions concerning the new "Community" between France and her former colonies (Arts. 77-87). They do constitute a great step in the right direction, and they have proven much more satisfactory, and much more flexible, than the equivalent provisions of the Constitution of the Fourth Republic. The actual nature of the relations between France and the former colonies will, however, be governed less by constitutional rules than by political factors which it is impossible to evaluate in advance.

CONSTITUTIONAL REVISION

A few words are, however, necessary concerning the provisions for changes in the constitution (Art. 89). The initiative may be taken by the President of the Republic on the proposal of the Prime Minister, or by members of parliament. In either case the revision must be adopted in identical terms by both houses. (This provision gives the Senate an absolute veto, which it did not have during either the Third or Fourth Republic (Art. 85), but which it seems unlikely to abuse.) Ordinarily, amendments become final only after having been approved in a referendum. This is, however, not the case when the President of the Republic submits a proposed amendment to a joint session of Assembly and Senate, and if three-fifths of those voting on it do so favorably.

This procedure is, on the whole, rather flexible. It is more difficult than that which prevailed under the Third Republic, but at that time no serious revision was possible because the simple majorities needed for that purpose could not be found. As long as the Fifth Republic combines majority voting with an effective right of dissolution, it seems likely that political leadership will be strong enough to secure the adoption of reforms for which there is a recognized need.

Besides, the government has all the powers which it could wish; where their extent goes too far they can, as mentioned above, in most cases, be modified by practical usage, without any explicit change of the constitution.

There are two exceptions to this rule, the first of which is the incompatibility between parliamentary mandate and membership in the government. If the above analysis is correct, the sooner this provision is abolished the better. This change the deputies and senators, if asked to do so, would adopt with an alacrity which, one hopes, does not indicate willingness to resume the old "hunt for portfolios."

The other change concerns the right of dissolution. This is the one case in which the constitution does not do enough to strengthen the executive since, once a dissolution has taken place, there cannot be another one until a year after the new elections. The intention is to make it impossible to dissolve a newly-elected Assembly before it can bring about the installation of a government which its majority desires. The ghost of the Weimar Republic inspired the fear that an untrammelled right of parliamentary dissolution might be abused. In 1932 Chancellor von Papen had announced calmly that the opposition of the Reichstag to his government did not bother him; he would simply allow that body to "vote itself to death"—whenever a new Reichstag was elected he would dissolve it before it was able to adopt a motion of censure. He could not entertain such thoughts, however, until a situation had arisen (made possible by P.R.) in which the Reichstag no longer contained a positive majority. A combination of opposites, including the Nazis and the Communists, was always able to overthrow a cabinet without having a chance to replace it. It is one thing to dissolve a parliament which is so clearly incapable of functioning that it lacks popular respect, and something else again to do this to one which has a positive majority, and is supported by the people.

The authors of the new constitution would have done better to direct their eyes across the British Channel, and across the oceans to the Commonwealth countries, rather than across the Rhine. Where the

English type of constitutional government prevails, dissolution is possible from the first moment of a parliament to its last. This is an essential part of the political action pattern. The rank and file of the "back-benchers" know that they must always support their leaders if they are not to risk an immediate dissolution. The government (meaning, in recent decades, the prime minister) may request a dissolution at any time and for any reason, be it a conflict between the cabinet and its supporters, or the assumption that conditions are most favorable for the majority party, or simply the wish to terminate the existence of a parliament which, having come close to the end of its term, is too election-minded to concentrate on its work.

In France such an unlimited type of parliamentary dissolution would be of particular significance. There will, for a long time, be nothing resembling a genuine two-party system. As a result a new prime minister will always find himself in a comparatively weak position. If he is at the mercy of the deputies for an entire year much of his authority will be frittered away; an action pattern which implies the consistent support of the cabinet by its majority will not easily evolve. What was accepted as a reasonable safeguard against executive overbearance may well prove the gate through which it will be possible to reintroduce the Trojan horse of a "government by assembly" in the French political system.[105]

THE ELECTORAL SYSTEM

In regard to the right of dissolution, then, the framers of the new French constitution stopped short of their logical goal. The same applies to the choice of the electoral system although, in this case, a measure of compromise was inevitable.

Ordinarily, it would have been necessary to discuss the electoral system before taking up the details of the constitution. The method of election has much to do with the structure of a country's political parties, as is demonstrated by the difference between the multiple system of related parties characteristic of the majority system with unlimited second ballot used during the Third Republic, and that of unrelated parties characteristic of the system of P.R. used during the Fourth Republic. The functioning of parliamentary government, in turn, depends upon the structure of political parties. If this is as favorable as it is under a two-party system, almost any written constitution will work, with the exception that it would not be safe to omit the right of dissolution. If the party system is as unfavorable as it is with a multiple system of unrelated parties (in particular when this is supplemented by strong extremist groups), even the best written constitution cannot make parliamentary government work.

The Fifth Republic did not, however, begin its career with a full-fledged parliamentary system. The policy of General de Gaulle overshadowed both parliament and parties. Nearly a century ago it was said that where there existed both a government and a parliament it was necessary that either the parliament should be able to "make" the government, or that the government should be able to "make" the parliament. There was a time when kings could do the latter, but it has long since passed. General de Gaulle was, however, able to do just that; most of the members of the National Assembly elected in November 1958 owed their success to their presumed willingness to place support for him above everything else. This meant that, for the time being, the composition of the Assembly, and the share of the electoral system in bringing it about, were comparatively unimportant.

The method of voting was, however, vitally important in a different way. In de Gaulle's rise to power the threat of insurrection formed so much of the background that the legitimacy of his rule seemed questionable. This changed when in the referendum of September 28, instead of the 60 per cent expected, nearly 80 per cent of the voters in "metropolitan" France supported the new constitution. The principle of a referendum is, of course, that of an unequivocal majority decision. The people are given a clear choice between "yes" and "no"; they are not invited to disperse behind one of any number of groups based on ideology or interest. Rudolf Smend[106] termed a majority decision, "a struggle with a tendency toward integration." He compared voting to an athletic contest: In both cases the outcome is, even for the loser, accompanied by "a beneficial discharge of tensions, a catharsis." This is what France had not known since its Liberation, and what it did experience overwhelmingly in September, 1958.

The decisive change in systems of voting, then, did not occur with the elections to the National Assembly of November 23 and 30; it occurred with the referendum of September 28. This was true in particular also because the very feature which was so often said to be a drawback of this vote was one of its greatest assets: The people were more interested in expressing their confidence in de Gaulle than in endorsing a constitution which few had read. Such a personal endorsement of a political leader, achieved in a vote which was free in all essentials, had that typical result of a majority verdict that minority and majority alike accepted it as a true community decision. Under these conditions the elections to the National Assembly were anti-climactic. For the people they constituted little more than a repetition of the referendum; once again they expressed their confidence in the General.

Future Assembly elections are unlikely to stand under the shadow of so popular a figure; they will, once again, follow their own dynamics in the guiding of which the electoral system will play its part.

That electoral systems are important has never been doubted by the leading constitutional experts of the Gaullist movement. Reference has been made to the vigorous opposition to P.R. offered by René Capitant[107] during the sessions of the first Constituent Assembly. Michel Debré, in his introduction to the draft of a new constitution prepared on behalf of the General Committee of Studies for the Resistance Council,[108] wrote: "Majority voting is retained and every thought of proportional representation is banished because [that system] confuses even the soundest political ideas and destroys any majority." After P.R. was adopted, Debré remained its most vigorous critic, emphasizing, in particular, "the decisive influence which a bad institution can have upon the manner in which people react."[109] He added that whereas majority voting tended to set limits to the elements of division within a country, P.R. encouraged them and threatened "the mental equilibrium of a nation."[110] Debré differed, however, from the traditional French advocates of majority voting in two respects. First, he wanted the plurality system, considering the second ballot a step in the direction of P.R. Second, he felt that, if the French tendency to political parochialism was to be overcome, there had to be multiple-member constituencies; they alone would assure the preponderance of truly national issues.

The introduction of such a system is, however, one thing if undertaken after a prolonged period of majority voting in single-member constituencies; it is something else again after P.R. has been used for more than a decade, destroying the ties which had existed among the parties of the moderate Right and Left and facilitating an increase in the extremist vote. As long as, in particular, the Communists control a substantial part of the electorate, plurality elections in single-member constituences are bound to give them a larger number of seats than is to be expected with a second ballot, even if this number is likely to be below what the Communists would gain under P. R. In the case of plurality elections in multiple-member constituencies the position of the Communists would have been more difficult; some of their local strongholds were certain to have been submerged in wider areas. What the Communists stood to lose was, however, likely to go almost entirely to the Right. The latter's tickets would have swept even larger parts of the country with mere pluralities in large multiple-member constituencies than they were to do in single-member constituencies.

These are the reasons why the traditional French system with a second ballot was advocated by various groups, such as the Radicals, the Socialists,[111] and many members of the moderate Right. The Communists, of course, wanted P.R. The M.R.P. would have preferred the modified P.R. system of 1951, hoping that enough *apparentements* could be concluded to reduce Communist (and possible Poujadist) strength, without jeopardizing the chances of the M.R.P. which were held to be small under majority voting.

The final decision lay with General de Gaulle. He wanted to avoid anything which would create the impression that he favored the right wing among his supporters, in particular the U.N.R., to the detriment of the others. At the same time he preferred a "clear and simple system"[112]; he knew that if the people had been given a choice among several methods, majority voting in single-member districts, with a second ballot, would have been the winner.

If these considerations favored the old system of majority voting[113] there yet remained the possibility of "moralizing" the second ballot. Something could be done to limit the possibilities of maneuvering between the two ballots. Various steps in this direction were taken.

Thus, it was provided that only the candidates participating in the first ballot could run in the second whereas, under the old rules, new candidates had been able to present themselves.

Furthermore, a small step was taken in a direction which, if pursued more actively, could have led to a higher degree of political concentration; candidates who obtained less than five per cent of the votes in the first ballot were eliminated from the second. A requirement of 15 per cent would have been preferable; it would have given two major candidates each of the Right and of the Left a chance to get into the second ballot, but reduced the leeway for maneuvering. Similar considerations apply to another innovation: Candidates had to make a deposit of 100,000 francs which was refunded if they obtained at least 5 per cent of the votes in the first ballot; the corresponding English requirement is 12.5 per cent, and France might at least have called for ten. Finally, candidates obtaining five per cent of the vote had certain campaign expenditures refunded to them, such as the cost of paper, the printing of ballots, and the cost of posters and circulars. *Le Figaro* estimated the amount at 500,000 francs,[114] at that time close to $1200. This privilege could also have been reserved for candidates obtaining a higher percentage.

The next major step on the road to promoting political concentration would have been simple run-off elections, limited to the two top men of the first ballot; under that system there can be no deals after the first ballot. In France it was feared that extremist candidates would frequently secure one of the top positions, or even both. The extent of this fear was affected by what the Germans call "milkmaid's arithmetic": It was assumed that the votes would be distributed as they had been under the old system. Actually, run-off elections promote a tendency for related parties to present common candidates in the *first* ballot. Moderate parties find it comparatively easy to combine with others, but it is one of the characteristics of extremists that they are exclusive, and can rarely win allies.[115] As a result, the chance of moderate candidates to top the field under a system of run-off elections is substantially better than would appear from the percentages which they obtain under a system with an unrestricted second ballot.[116] There would be reasons to go farther in the direction of promoting political concentration; as a matter of fact, a time-table might have been drawn up for the gradual establishment in successive elections, first of run-off elections, and, ultimately, of the plurality system.

The mood prevailing in this respect in the France of 1958 was, however, one of "safety first," and "safety" was judged on the basis of the experience made with the unrestricted second ballot during the Third Republic as well as in the "cantonal elections" held during the Fourth. For a number of reasons,[117] the outcome of the latter gives only a rough indication of what might have happened had the same electoral system been used for the National Assembly, but certain broad conclusions can be drawn. The last "cantonal" elections of the Fourth Republic were held in April 1958, just a few weeks before the "Revolution of May." The Communists with 22.3% of the votes secured but 50 of the 1526 seats at stake; they lost 31 of the seats held previously. Those who, without being extremists in the proper sense of the term, stood farthest to the Right, the Social Republicans (they had been members of the Gaullist R.P.F.), secured only 64 seats, a loss of 18 with 3.5 per cent of the votes. The largest number of seats went to the centrist parties: The Radicals and various related groups had 387 seats (with 15.2 per cent of the votes), and the "Moderates" 522 seats (with 23.4 per cent of the votes).

Shaping the "Living Constitution"

The Assembly Elections

ON THIS BASIS IT WAS GENERALLY expected that the Assembly elections, while likely to give a large number of seats to the "Union for the New Republic," the U.N.R., which was led by the more ardent Gaullists, the lion's share would yet go to the Socialists, the Radicals and the "Moderates." The outcome was to be entirely different, with the U.N.R. obtaining so many seats that, together with the deputies from Algeria, it came close to having an over-all majority, with the Socialists and the Radicals losing heavily.

One reason for the unexpected result lay in the confusion characteristic of the campaign. All the old groups were in the race, and some of them had been subjected to a process of splintering. Besides, there were new ones, such as Georges Bidault's "Christian Democrats." During the Third Republic the habits of majority voting were well enough developed to keep such disintegrating tendencies in check. Thus in 1936, in the last elections to the old Chamber of Deputies, 185 out of 618 seats were filled with an absolute majority in the first ballot; in 1958 this happened only with 42 out of 465 seats in "metropolitan France." There was also a difference in campaign strategy. For 1936 Georges Lachapelle,[118] the Third Republic's leading electoral statistician and proponent of P.R., commented: "...the struggle which began during the first ballot in dispersion was continued in the second

with more discipline. The two opposing forces of the national front
and of the 'popular front'[119] united, as a rule, one against the other in
order to secure a plurality of the votes in the second ballot." In 1958
these habits of cooperation did not develop to a significant extent;
besides, the "presidential" character of the new political system made
it somewhat less imperative for parties to form coalitions in order to
secure a common majority. At any rate, the parliamentary correspondent of *Le Figaro*[120] remarked: "Uniform electoral strategy: that of
'Everyone for himself.'" Written in regard to the first ballot, this
heading characterized much of the second. The scattering of the votes
was so great that an unusual number of results was accidental.[121] The
following table[122] presents the over-all results:

ELECTIONS TO THE NATIONAL ASSEMBLY, November, 1958

Parties	Seats*		Votes					
	1958	1956	1958				1956	
			Second ballot		First ballot		(only one ballot)	
			Number	%age	Number	%age	Number	%age
Communists	10	145	3,741,384	20.7	3,882,204	18.9	5,532,631	25.7
Var. Leftists	2				347,298	1.4	449,472	2.0
Socialists	40	88	2,484,417	13.7	3,167,354	15.5	3,180,656	14.8
Radicals	13	56	362,784	2.0	983,201	4.8	2,876,398[1]	13.3
Left Center	22	18	1,035,625	5.7	1,364,788	6.7		
M.R.P. and Christ. Dem.	44-13	71	1,365,064	7.5	2,378,788	11.6	2,374,221	11.0
U.N.R.	188	16[2]	4,769,052	26.4	3,603,958	17.6	948,854	4.4
Moderates	120-12	95	4,250,539	23.6	4,092,600	19.9	3,086,414	14.3
Ext. Right	1	52			669,518	3.3	2,816,805[3]	13.1
TOTAL	440-25	541	18,008,865	99.6	20,489,709	99.7	21,265,451	98.6

*The number of seats in metropolitan France was reduced from 544 in 1956
  to 465 in 1958.
[1]With Dissident Radicals and Left Center.
[2]"Social Republicans" in 1956.
[3]Including the Poujadists.

The great victor of the elections, the U.N.R., benefitted substantially from the more than 1.6 million votes lost by the Communists.
Most of these did not, as one might have expected, go to the Socialists;
a sizable number moved all the way to the Right. With the help of this
windfall the U.N.R. had surprised itself in the first ballot. Their leaders

decided to "go all out" for the second, even in cases where a Rightist, and pro-Gaullist, candidate was leading in the first, and in some cases even where a Communist might be the beneficiary of such a decision. It was felt that, since the voters had by then been "enlightened" as to the true chances of the U.N.R. many of them would support its candidates on the second ballot who had not done so in the first. The expectation proved correct; the U.N.R. achieved a substantial increase in popular strength between November 23 and 30. The Independents ("Moderates") did less well, but the fact that, together with the U.N.R., they polled 50 per cent of the votes cast in the second ballot should at least modify the claim that the majority in the National Assembly consisting of these two groups misrepresented the will of the country.

Still, the unexpected success of the U.N.R. created its problems. It was a rather heterogeneous group. Critics estimated that perhaps one third of its deputies were real Gaullists; one third were in favor of "authoritarian" government, more Pétainist than Gaullist;[123] one third were opportunists who jumped on the Gaullist bandwagon. During the months which followed upon the elections the moderate and genuinely Gaullist element came to prevail, but the more radical members of the U.N.R.'s parliamentary group made their presence felt; in some of their demands they were supported by the majority of the Algerian deputies and by a part of the Independents. What made the position of the moderate Gaullists at all tenable was the right of dissolution which President de Gaulle was willing to use as soon as there should be a serious deviation from his program. Since more than half of the U.N.R. seats were marginal, this threat was highly effective.

When evaluating the over-all results of the elections it is helpful to consider how the seats would have been distributed if their number had been exactly proportional to the number of votes obtained. This calculation presupposes, of course, that the votes would have been cast under P.R. as they were in the first ballot of the majority elections. This assumption is not entirely correct; it ignores, in particular, the substantial swing toward the U.N.R. in the second ballot. Also, the complete proportionality assumed between votes and seats never obtained under French election laws. Still, the figures [124] are not without interest:

Parties	Seats with P.R.	Seats Actually Obtained
Communists	88	10
Socialists	72	40
Various Leftists	8	2
Radicals	23	13
Left Center	31	22
M.R.P. and Christian Democracy	42	57
U.N.R.	82	189
Moderates (Independents)	94	132
Extreme Right	15	1

One of the lessons to be drawn from these figures is that whenever candidates openly campaigned under an extremist banner (the U.N.R. claimed to be moderate, even centrist) they suffered a disastrous defeat. The Communists secured only ten seats instead of 88, but the "extreme Right" (mostly Poujadists) suffered percentagewise even more, obtaining one seat instead of 15. Under the majority system Rightist groups of this kind find it difficult to recover from such a setback. P.R., on the other hand, would have left them with a nucleus sufficient to attract further strength. They might have been joined by those members of the U.N.R. who were critical of de Gaulle's Algerian policy and resented "the remnants of the system" — the continued existence of political parties other than their own.

If the defeat of the extremists of the Right was overwhelming in terms of seats, that of the Communists mattered more in view of the numbers involved. Naturally, the Communist daily, *L'Humanité*,[125] complained bitterly of the electoral system, and the Communist press the world over joined in the outcry. A good many non-Communist French were inclined to feel the same way. Yet a democratic parliament has no place for a large number of members whose only intention is to wreck it from within. When Madison, in No. 10 of *The Federalist*, emphasized that the majority principle helps to "break and control the violence of faction," he admitted that such a group might yet be strong enough "to convulse the society," but it would, at least "be unable to execute and mask its violence under the forms of the Constitution." This is the chance which the French Communists lost in November 1958, and it is a chance which they never should have had. On the other hand, the Communists were not denied the opportunity to express their views. Whatever they had to say, ten of them could say as well as the 88. When, in 1857, the Republican opposition to Napoleon III elected its first five deputies, their speeches had a powerful impact upon the country. Ten Communists could have accomplished the same in the first popularly elected parliament of the Fifth Republic if they had had a message. Actually, the speeches of the Communist deputies had always been limited to a repetition of the party line's stereotypes. In the fulfillment of this task the 150 Communists and "Progressives" elected in 1956 could hardly do more than the ten deputies elected in 1958, whose number did not matter, therefore, so far as contributions to parliamentary deliberations are concerned.

Nor did the reduction of the Communist representation in the National Assembly constitute a misrepresentation of the voters' wishes. It has been ascertained by every conceivable test, in particular public opinion polls, that at least half of the French Communist voters have no intention of endorsing a totalitarian system; their only wish is to register a protest. If the majority system prevents such votes from being used to undermine democracy, it does no more than to protect the actual preferences of these electors.

Ultimately, the French political system cannot, of course, function properly unless the Communist popular vote is reduced. In 1958 it seemed that a substantial beginning had been made in this direction. The Communists were aware that the decline in their popular vote, which reached 1.5 million on November 23, was due to the majority system. As *L'Humanité*[126] put it the day after the elections: "The system of voting has been chosen precisely because it was most apt to reduce not only our representation but also our suffrages."

Yet, this result was not to prove lasting. In the long run, it is unlikely that votes lost by the Communists can be absorbed, and assimilated, by a party like the U.N.R. These are leftist votes: if they do not go to the moderate Left, in particular the Socialists, they are likely to return to the extreme Left. In 1958 the democratic Left appeared unattractive. It had been discredited by the fact that the policy of the coalition governments which it supported was not its own, although there was no alternative to this course of action if the Repulic was not to collapse. In November 1958 the psychological situation of the Socialists continued to be difficult. Guy Mollet and several other Socialist leaders were members of de Gaulle's cabinet; thus, their party could not present a policy of its own. The Socialists did manage to secure about the same percentage of the popular vote which they held in 1956. This was, however, not enough for them to gain even the number of seats which corresponded to their percentage of the popular vote; instead of 72 seats they secured only 40. This was a reversal of the precedent set in the last case in which the majority system had been used in national elections; in 1936 the Socialists had, for the first time, won a higher percentage of the seats than of the votes. It seemed that, henceforth, they would be among the beneficiaries of majority voting. Political prognosticators, in fact, accorded the Socialists something like 100 seats in the new National Assembly. They failed to take into account the damage which 12 years of P.R. had done to the Socialist party which, as mentioned above, while polling at least as many votes (and several times as many seats) as the Communists in the municipal and cantonal elections of 1945, had fallen behind the Communists in terms of both votes and seats as soon as P.R. was adopted.

Still, when the Socialists fared as badly as they did and the U.N.R. developed as the great victor this was bound to lead to a revival of Communist popular strength. One extreme strengthens the other, and the U.N.R. was, rightly or wrongly, regarded as a party of the extreme Right. The trend towards a revival of the Communist popularity began, in fact, with the second ballot of the Assembly elections. *L'Humanité*[127] was able to announce proudly that, in one week, the Communist candidates had regained 120,000 votes in the Paris region alone. If this happened at a time when it was as yet hardly possible for a reaction to the rise of the U.N.R. to develop it was bound to happen at an accelerated pace later, all the more so since new factors developed which operated to the advantage of the Communists.

ECONOMIC POLICY

Within a few weeks after the Assembly elections, the French political scene was to be changed profoundly by the new economic policies promulgated by the then Prime Minister de Gaulle. The

General remembered that when, on the morning of his country's Liberation, his Minister of Finance, Pierre Mendés-France, submitted to him a program designed to end inflation, he had rejected it in favor of a more opportunistic policy. In 1958 he was determined not to repeat such a mistake and decided on a policy of "verity and severity." It was to enable France to meet her national and international obligations without further inflation.

There were good reasons for this decision. A strong inflationary trend had developed in France since the end of the war. Attempts were made to hide its consequences by providing subsidies for certain products, and by manipulating the cost of living index. Such measures could not, however, prevent a serious deterioration of French foreign trade. The country imported substantially more than it exported and lost, within 18 months, close to two billion dollars in foreign exchange.

There were several schools of thought as to what should be done.[128] The Left favored a policy of expansion; it argued that increased production would make it possible to meet the country's commitments, and, in particular, to avoid a recession. A policy of this kind was also favored at the Right; Albin Chalandon, who was to become Secretary General of the U.N.R., had expressed himself in this sense. The great drawback of this policy was that, whatever else it might accomplish, it risked aggravating rather than mitigating the crisis of foreign exchange. It was certainly inflationary in the short run; the inflationary forces, once released, might not have been easy to check later.

An intermediate position was taken by Finance Minister Pinay who, apparently, would have preferred a policy similar to the one which had proven so successful when he was Prime Minister in 1952. There would have been no substantial reduction in expenditures or increase in taxes. Pinay hoped that the return of French capital invested abroad (or hoarded inside the country to the tune of three to four thousand tons of gold, equivalent to three to four billion dollars) would solve the crisis of foreign exchange. The remaining problems would take care of themselves in the course of time.

General de Gaulle and his advisers felt that a program of the type favored by Pinay would not solve his country's problems; it would only postpone them. Therefore, they accepted a plan prepared by a group of experts, headed by the well-known economist, Professor Jacques Rueff. It contemplated halving the expected budgetary deficit of 1200 billion francs, on the assumption that 600 billion could be financed by genuine savings. Three hundred billion francs were to be gained by cutting down expenditures and another 300 billion by increased taxation. At the same time, the franc was to be devalued in order to make certain that French products were no longer overpriced abroad.

The authors of this policy have been charged with placing monetary policy above everything else, and forgetting the need for economic expansion. They vigorously denied the latter charge, emphasizing that a sound recovery could take place only on the basis of a reasonably stable price level; there had been such a recovery in Germany.

In France, a renewal of economic expansion could not be expected immediately but, admittedly, the monetary purposes of the program were achieved quickly and brilliantly. In the past no devaluation of the French franc had been a success; if it lowered the price of French products on foreign markets, this was soon offset by an increase in costs. On this occasion the increase in prices was kept to about 4 per cent, well within the limits contemplated, and equally within the limits of what France could afford in order to remain competitive in foreign markets. The balance of trade improved forthwith, and the balance of payments even more; a significant amount of capital did return from its foreign and domestic hiding places. The French franc became, almost overnight, a "hard" currency; by the middle of 1959 it was stronger on international markets than the dollar.

Yet, there remained the economic and the psychological problem. The question was whether the light recession which had begun to develop in the early months of 1958, before de Gaulle took over, could be checked. In our day people are no longer satisfied if major depressions are avoided; they want continuous economic progress. In France the onset of relative stagnation did reduce the purchasing power of a large number of workers. Wages had been falling behind the increase in prices for some time and workers suffered even more substantial losses on account of the decline in working hours. Small pockets of unemployment developed. Insignificant by comparison with other countries and with the French economy as a whole, they loomed large in the public eye and served as the catalyzer of a substantial political agitation. This was the case in spite of all indication that the economic decline would not last, and that, while improvement might be slow for a time, it was unlikely to be delayed for long. Such economic prospects belong, however, too much to the range of "long term" considerations to affect the political thinking of the average person.

Problems also arose on account of the government's failure to prepare the people for its policies. While the over-all proposals of the Rueff plan were excellent, they were not the ones people expected, or which the political leaders of the majority would have adopted if acting on their own. Ultimately, the advantages of the new policy might become obvious to all but, in the meantime, there was bound to be discontent. Certainly, de Gaulle's policy of "verity and severity" differed substantially in its psychological aspects from its German counterpart, the "social market policy." While Professor Erhard was an academic economist, he had also the talents of a political leader. Whenever he proved a little slow in making politically advisable concessions, his chief, that consummate political artist, Chancellor Adenauer, set matters right. De Gaulle's economic advisers lacked the acumen of the political leader. The experts "proposed" and the General "disposed," leaving the Debré government (which took over a few days after the enactment of these measures), somewhat unhappily in the middle. Not having devised the new policy its members did not quite know how to explain it.

To compound these difficulties the program included two measures which were all but insignificant from the economic point of view, but psychologically disastrous. First, the rather small pensions which all veterans drew, whether disabled or not, were cancelled. General de Gaulle had said that the veterans would be called upon to give up voluntarily those benefits which were not based on actual disability. Two days later, the "technocracy" (the mixture of bureaucrats and economic experts), who did not know how to cope with such voluntary arrangements, abolished these pensions by a stroke of the pen, although those based on actual disabilities were raised. The resultant psychological reaction was a boon to the adversaries of the new government.

A second step had similar effects. In the past the French social system had refunded to its members all of their expenses for medicines. Henceforth, this was to be done only for the amount exceeding 3,000 francs (a little more than $6.00) every six months. The loss in purchasing power involved was somewhat more serious than the cancellation of the veterans' pensions; large families definitely suffered. Even so, the economic effects of this measure — repealed during the summer of 1959 — were minor by comparison with the ones caused by the reduction of working hours, which could not, however, be dramatized with equal facility.

The impression of technocratic and bureaucratic rule was strengthened by the flood of reforms which were decreed during the last weeks of the year. Most of them were long overdue; plans had been drawn up by the men of the Fourth Republic who could not get them adopted. Once again, however, the public had not been prepared. Besides, some of these measures contained provisions typical of their bureaucratic origin which proper political control could have eliminated.

As matters developed, there soon spread a general feeling of *malaise*. The government had accomplished much but had also caused some avoidable friction. There were many who eagerly used any pretext in order to embarrass a government which they could not challenge outright. The more moderate critics could not, of course, rival the Communists who had the advantage that their opposition appeared genuine, since they were the only major group which had opposed de Gaulle from the start, and they cashed in heavily on their opportunity.

THE MUNICIPAL ELECTIONS

The first indication of how these factors affected French politics appeared in elections for the departmental councils (*élections cantonales*) and for the National Assembly which became necessary because the election of several deputies had been invalidated. The Communist vote[129] increased markedly; there were indications that the popular front tactics which had been virtually absent from the Assembly elections in November had regained a limited measure of popularity.

The trend was accentuated in the municipal elections. Purely local and personal considerations played their part in them, but there is agreement that, taken as a whole, the elections did demonstrate a marked change in French national politics. The system of voting had been altered.[130] In the past towns with less than 9,000 inhabitants had used the majority system (with two ballots) and the larger ones P.R. This time the majority system was extended to all cities with less than 120,000 inhabitants. Candidates, who ran at large, were elected on the first ballot if they secured an absolute majority; otherwise, there was a second ballot in which the remaining seats went to those who obtained the highest vote.

It is difficult to summarize the over-all results of these elections. Parties did not present candidates everywhere and, at times, they presented them together with others.[131] Figures are most easily comparable in the case of those cities which voted under P.R. both on the occasion of the preceding municipal elections, held in 1953, and of the ones of 1959.[132] They show that the general tendency was for the Communists to regain the votes lost during the Assembly elections, and for the U.N.R. and the Independents to suffer corresponding losses. In these cities the Communist percentage of the popular vote increased from 18.9 in the Assembly elections to 24.9.

The Communists captured several additional municipalities, notably in the Paris area, which they had not controlled in the preceding municipal elections, held in 1953. In the country at large they lost a significant number of seats as the following tabulation of the Ministry of the Interior demonstrates:[133]

Distribution of Seats in the Municipal Councils of Metropolitan France.

Parties	Outgoing	Elected	Difference
Communists	24,206	20,454	—3,752
Various Leftists	35,625	28,603	—7,022
Socialists	58,382	52,145	—6,237
Radicals and Related Groups	48,796	39,405	—9,391
Center and Left Center	60,244	59,125	—1,119
U.N.R.	16,958	22,253	+ 5,295
M.R.P.	35,950	32,347	—3,603
Moderates and Independents (Rightists)	167,726	169,840	+ 2,114
Local Lists	21,713	43,893	+22,180
Extreme Right	1,387	1,416	+ 29
Total	470,987	469,481	

The principal conclusion to be drawn from these figures is that of a "return to normalcy." The typical effects of majority elections appeared in the over-all distribution of seats, but this time the U.N.R. could not, as had been the case in the Assembly elections, manage to be the principal beneficiary of majority voting. The moderate Rightists did best, but the moderate Left did secure enough seats to indicate that, had the Assembly elections been held in March, the Socialists and the Radicals would have pushed the U.N.R. into the background.

Meanwhile, the great problem of French politics remained *le fait communiste* — the fact that, once again, something like a fourth of all voters had supported the candidates of the extreme Left. This fact not only deprived the moderate Left of a support on which it could otherwise have counted, but it divided the total left-wing vote so much that, in many cases, Rightist candidates secured their seats by mere pluralities. The French political system will not be healthy unless there is a marked change in this respect. A condition must be reached again in which the moderate Left has a chance to secure a parliamentary majority of its own. For this reason the Communist vote need not disappear; it would be adequate if the Socialists would regain the parity with the Communists which they held in the municipal and cantonal elections of 1945. In that case the number of Socialist seats would, in national as well as in local elections, be sufficient to make them a large parliamentary power, capable of obtaining a majority in alliance with other left-wing groups, excluding the Communists.

Ultimately, then, everything depends on the Socialists regaining enough of their popular prestige to win over, let us say, one-fourth of the present Communist vote. If majority elections continue and the Socialists remain free from government responsibility for some years, they should be able to solve this task. It would facilitate matters if the bickering which developed between Guy Mollet and his opponents, in particular the "autonomous Socialists," would cease. When, after the 1956 elections, Mollet compromised the traditional stand of his party, in particular in regard to Algeria, the reason was not a personal preference; there was no way to govern France legally except if the Socialists participated in governments together with the Right. The necessity for such a combination has now ceased; the question is how long its psychological effects will last.

A policy aiming at a rebuilding of Socialist strength would, of course, have to reject any attempt to form a new "popular front." The official leaders of the party have done so, but they have not always been followed by the rank and file. In the municipal elections of 1959 there were 75 cases of "popular front" tickets in the 411 towns with more than 9000 inhabitants. In 36 cases none[134] of the candidates on these lists were elected; of 29 but a small number were elected, but 19 were successful enough to elect either the entire membership of a municipal council or its majority. All of this was serious enough to cause concern, but far from being alarming. The over-all results showed clearly that the Socialists, rejecting alliances at their Left, will always be able to take the measure of the Communists in terms of seats. This happened although the Socialist vote was comparatively small; it would be very much more the case if the Socialists made perceptible gains.

Some Socialist leaders have nevertheless demanded the adoption of P.R.; one of the reasons given is that this would reduce the pressure for a "popular front." It is overlooked that a return to P.R. would re-introduce the very factor which caused the decline in post-war Socialist popularity; their parliamentary group would, once again, have to co-operate with the Right in the formation of governments. On the other hand, while it may take time under a majority system for the Socialists to regain a part of the votes lost to the Communists since 1945, there would appear to be a good enough chance for this to be done, provided that the Socialists play their cards properly.

THE SENATE ELECTIONS

If the municipal elections represented a certain "return to normalcy," the Senate elections of April 26 continued the trend. This was a foregone conclusion. The election of the senators was indirect, as during the Third and Fourth Republics. A separate electoral college meets in each *département*. It consists of the local deputies, the members of the departmental councils, the members of municipal councils, and of additional delegates elected by the councils of the larger cities.

The *départements* which elected no more than four senators did so under the majority system: In the first ballot a candidate was successful if he secured an absolute majority of the votes cast (as well as 25 per cent of the total number of voters). In the second ballot, which took place on the afternoon of the same day, a plurality decided. In most of these cases majority rule applied at least twice; the municipal councils had been elected under the majority system, and they, plus the delegates chosen by them, voted for the senators under majority rule. This is the reason why centrist parties, in particular the Radicals, have always done well in these elections, and why the extremists, be they of the Left or of the Right, have done poorly.

In the seven *départements* which were entitled to five or more senators the respective electoral colleges (composed of members chosen on the basis of P.R. and in part on the basis of the majority system) voted under P.R. The largest of them, the *Département Seine,* which includes Paris, elected 22 senators; altogether 60 of the 255 senators to be elected in "metropolitan France" were chosen under P.R.

The following table[135] gives the over-all results as compared with the last Council of the Republic (which had 246 members for "metropolitan France"):

Communists	14	—2
Socialists	48	—5
Radicals and Related Groups	52	+5
U.N.R. (formerly Social Republicans)	27	—2
M.R.P.	29	+8
Independents and Peasants	85	+5

It will be seen that the changes were small.[136] The greatest gains were made by the M.R.P., which had strengthened its "infrastructure" in the municipal elections. The U.N.R. not only failed to match the striking gains made in November but actually lost two of the seats held by the "Social Republicans." By this time the U.N.R.'s strength had declined sufficiently to give it fewer seats under majority voting than it would have received under P.R. So far as the Communists are concerned, all of their 14 seats were gained under P.R. This does not mean that they would have secured no seats at all under a majority system; one estimate accords them five or six in that case.[137] At any rate once again it became clear that the majority system will, in the normal course of events, favor moderate parties.

In order to illustrate the contrast in the composition of the National Assembly and the Senate it is well to compare the percentage of the membership won by the various groups:

	Senate	National Assembly
Communists	5.5	2.5
Socialists	18.5	9
Radicals and related groups	20	7.5
U.N.R.	11	43
M.R.P.	11.5	11
Independents and Peasants	33.5	27

Clearly, in the Senate the moderate Left and Center predominate as much as the U.N.R. and the Independents do in the Assembly. The comparative gain of the Communists in the Senate is, of course, due to P.R.

From the point of view of long-term trends the Senate appears as a more "legitimate" body than the Assembly, in which the large number of U.N.R. deputies reflects a mere accident. Party strength in the Senate comes closer to what the French political picture is likely to be in the future, although allowance must be made for the overlarge weight wielded in senatorial elections by the small communities. Furthermore, many of the abler leaders of the Fourth Republic who had been defeated when running for the Assembly entered the Senate, providing that body with a preponderance of talent and experience. The Assembly, in addition, saw its deliberative character weakened when deputies of the Left or the Center who criticized the official Algerian policy, or even the policy advocated by the "integrationist" extremists, were shouted down, whereas in the Senate everybody was given a hearing and the procedure remained dignified. The Senate may not be able to rival the powers of the Assembly but it will, apparently, maintain the traditions of a respected parliamentary body. Also, it seems destined to disappoint those who had wanted it to be powerful in the expectation that it would strengthen the hand of the government; it opposed, on more than one occasion, the cabinet with a vigor unthinkable on the part of a National Assembly subject to dissolution. The government had reason to congratulate itself that the powers of the new Senate were less extensive than those of its predecessor during the Third Republic, which had possessed an absolute power of veto in matters of legislation.

THE FIFTH REPUBLIC AND THE FUTURE

WITH THE ELECTION OF THE Senate the major institutions of the Fifth Republic had been constituted, and the question is how they can be expected to work. The first consideration is that the Assembly elections operated as a serious obstacle to the institutionalization of political power. That institutionalization would, normally, have led to an increase in the significance of the parliamentary features of the new constitution over the presidential ones. Given the result of the November elections such a development would have led to policies unlikely to be accepted by the country. Had the majority consisting of the U.N.R., the Algerian deputies, and the right wing of the Independents been left to itself it would have insisted on a strict "integration" of Algeria with France. Such a policy would not only have jeopardized any chance of a peaceful settlement with the Algerian nationalists, but it would also have built up additional tensions within France herself. Under these circumstances the more responsible Liberal observers argued that it was inopportune to insist upon the rights of parliament as against those of the President. De Gaulle offered the only hope for a moderate policy in regard to Algeria; also, his sincere intention to maintain his country's basic liberties was known. Dependence upon the President became, therefore, even greater than could have been expected according to the constitution; Maurice Duverger, who had warned against stressing the powers of the new Assembly as against those of the President, found it necessary to conclude: "A man has replaced the state."[138] Still, reliance on the President appeared natural as long as the more important branch of parliament was out of tune with the country's basic political orientation, which de Gaulle did reflect.

A strengthening of the truly institutional elements in the Fifth Republic would also require the development of an acceptable pattern of parliamentary action. If there was agreement that the "parliamentary manners" of the Third and Fourth Republics had to change and that the deputies needed to be "reeducated," it was no less clear that the solution of that task required the willing cooperation of the more responsible deputies and senators. Their position was difficult enough because many of their colleagues did, and still do, hanker after the fleshpots of power and profit on which they feasted during the Third and Fourth Republics. The separation of the parliamentary wheat from the chaff was, however, not facilitated when parliament as a whole was subjected to so many restrictions that all of its members felt slighted; rightly or wrongly, the impression gained ground that the position of parliament was to be lowered even more than was contemplated by the constitution.

The immediate occasion for conflict was the matter of the "oral questions" which, according to Art. 48 of the constitution, were to be asked once a week. This is a weapon which the then Senator Michel Debré had handled adroitly while a member of the Council of the Republic and which he felt could be a useful tool in the constructive control of the government by parliament. He would not have objected (or at least would not have been able to object) were this institution to be used as it is used in England, although there, too, its function is as much to embarrass the government as it is to elicit information.[139] There developed a serious clash, however, when the provisional rules of the Assembly (and the ones finally adopted by the Senate) provided for the possibility of a vote after a question.

It seemed to Debré — and to many others — that the French deputies and senators wanted to do more than engage in control of the government. They had been used to challenge cabinets by "interpellations": general debates which were followed by a vote and which not infrequently led to a defeat of the cabinet. The new constitution intended to rule out any such possibility; otherwise, the elaborate safeguards of Art. 49 would make no sense. Nor did some of the arguments advanced by the deputies and senators strengthen their case. They held, for example, that since there now existed a strong government it would not be damaged if parliament should vote against it on a particular issue. Debré quite rightly answered that action based on such principles would lead to constant "harassment" of the government, which would, if matters went far enough, be weakened to such an extent that it would have to resign.

The defenders of the proposed rule had a better case when they argued that what the government was afraid of was, ultimately, its own majority. For, if the latter stood by the government, there was nothing to fear. This was true enough but, then, the detailed provisions of the new constitution were based on the assumption that there would not be, for some time to come, any disciplined majority of the English type; deputies and senators were to be given as few opportunities to act irresponsibly as possible. This is a view which many neutral observers were inclined to accept,[140] and which the Constitutional Council endorsed when the rules were submitted to it in acordance with Art. 61 of the constitution.

That ruling, however, went farther than expected; it apparently made any and all kinds of parliamentary resolutions impossible. The only direct way in which the government can now be challenged is by a motion of censure, to be made by a tenth of the Assembly's members and to be endorsed by an absolute majority. If it is defeated its signatories cannot introduce another motion during the same session. This is one reason why even responsible observers have felt that while most of the restrictions on parliamentary initiative were necessary, others were definitely outside the accepted pattern of parliamentary life. A motion of censure should always be possible. Nor should the deputies and senators be deprived of the possibility of proposing a diminution of expenditures; this is one of the oldest rights of parliamentary assemblies.

Parliament retains, of course, the power of refusing its assent to new legislation and to appropriations, even if this right is now limited. Professor Duverger has argued that "within the framework imposed upon them the Chambers could find an important activity, close enough to that of the British parliament, under the condition of adapting themselves to the new rules of the game."[141] The question remains nevertheless whether the elaborate rules which now harness parliamentary work will prove successful in the long run, or whether, as predicted by Raymond Aron,[142] they will collapse. Like so many other features of the new constitution they owe their enforcement to General de Gaulle's popularity which, in turn, rests in part on the fact that he alone could eliminate the danger of revolution. It is a measure of General de Gaulle's devotion to his country's general welfare that he lost no time trying to eliminate the revolutionary atmosphere although its continuance gave him a position of indispensability without which his power was in danger of receding. As mentioned above, he moved decisively toward conciliation in regard to Tunisia a few weeks after having been installed as prime minister. To the Algerians he first offered a "peace of the brave," and when this was rejected, he went, in his speech of September 16, 1959, so far as to mention "independence" as one of the ways in which, abhorrent as it was to him and detrimental as it would be to Algerians and French alike, the conflict might be solved. There are few, if any, cases in French politics in which a political leader has acted with more courage, as the General's action was bound to be fiercely resented by some of those who had done most to bring him to power. He won new friends (or, rather confirmed the allegiance of old friends) at the Left and Center but these men represented tendencies which could not, in the long run, be expected to adhere to the Gaullist concept of government. De Gaulle acted with equal determination in regard to the army in Algeria. It had become a state within a state, and a well-informed journalist wrote of the views characteristic of many of its officers: "One encounters, on the other hand, the strong feeling that democracy was in itself the illness from which France suffered for so long. In the military mind here, 'Democracy' means the impotent rule of a divided Parliament. And reformed as it may be under the new constitution, one gathers that the National Assembly is still regarded by many officers as a relic of the old 'system' and a symptom of national weakness."[143] De Gaulle brought these feelings under control. Yet, gratitude has never been a characteristic of politics in any country. French politicians have repeatedly submitted to a strong leader under duress, only to reject him as soon as conditions had regained a measure of normalcy.

In the case of de Gaulle this will not be easy and it will not happen rapidly. Still, the assumption that he has institutionalized the high degree of power which he wielded both before and after the adoption of the new constitution is invalid. French political life as it developed under his guidance does not comply with the requirements of any regular pattern. As one French observer put it in conversation with the author: The Fifth Republic follows neither the lines of parliamentary, nor those of a presidential government: it is "superpresidential." President de Gaulle controls not only the executive, but also the legislature. He has for the time being been able to transcend the limitations of power set to his office under his own constitution, being able to count on the constitution being revised if that should be deemed necessary. Such powers are definitely of a "personal" rather than an "institutional" character. Realization of this fact is obscured by de Gaulle's view that the president is to be an "arbiter" who decides "impartially" between the political contestants just as a referee in an athletic struggle decides between two teams. If the analogy were correct, the position could be institutionalized. Actually, however, the political "arbiter" does not simply interpret a preestablished set of rules. His decisions are genuine political choices. Those who disagree are bound to oppose him, and this makes him a partisan against his will. It is interesting that the first ones to make this point and to state definitely that they were attacking the President rather than his Prime Minister were a group of Algerian deputies who had been among the most ardent champions of his return to power. For the time being their attacks on the President consolidated his support among the more moderate deputies, but many of the latter disagreed with him on other points, such as economic policy and the relations between parliament and government. In the Senate a majority was openly hostile to Prime Minister Debré. This meant, in fact, that it was opposed to de Gaulle. As matters stood in 1959 any newly-elected National Assembly was likely to contain a majority similar to that of the Senate. In that case a successful motion of censure would be directed as much against de

Gaulle as against Debré. Since, for a year after the elections following a dissolution, de Gaulle would be unable to proceed to a new dissolution, it is difficult to see how a defeat of his cabinet could permit him to stay in office and assert his old powers.

Any long-run solution of France's political problems must take these facts into account. Adequate executive authority cannot rest on the shoulders of one man. It must be based on genuine political forces which, to use an expression of Montesquieu, constitute a government's "intermediate powers." De Gaulle has attempted to rely on direct popular acclamation, and between him and the people there developed a political void. The General seemed to welcome it; he had little liking for political parties and felt that most of France's problems were of a technical and non-political nature. Yet, while a technical approach can be helpful in certain fields it is, in the long run, bound to prove insufficient. In a modern democracy any stable executive has to rest on organized political support, most of which must be derived from political parties. A party system capable of functioning is, therefore, a *conditio sine qua non* of an orderly constitutional life.

Some of France's most outstanding political writers have despaired of such a solution.[144] Professor Vedel was the first of several to point out that France's political divisions went so deep, that, in his view, the development of a responsible party system was so difficult that the Gordian knot had to be cut by adopting a presidential system on the American model. Subsequently, Professor Goguel endorsed this solution, and Professor Duverger modified it by suggesting that a prime minister (rather than the president) be elected directly by the people. According to this plan there was to be automatically a new election of both the parliament and the prime minister in case of a vote of censure. The goal, then, was more the reform than the abolition of the parliamentary system. Evidently, Duverger was anxious to secure for the French government that plebiscitary sanction which, as a result of the two-party system, a British prime minister now obtains automatically as a result of an election, the latest case being that of Mr. Macmillan in 1959.

The possible weaknesses of Duverger's plan arise from the very nature of the party system which it is intended to correct. With a system of multiple and unrelated parties, such as developed as a result of P.R. under the Fourth Republic, a candidate for the office of prime minister could not easily secure the support of a popular majority; as the choice of a mere plurality he would have a difficult task in a parliament dominated by parties opposing him. The situation would, of course, be different with majority voting for parliamentary elections (which Duverger advocates). In that case, it would at least be possible that the type of coalition similar to the *cartel des gauches* of 1924, or to the "popular front" of 1936, would elect both a prime minister and a parliamentary majority. Such a development could prove to be a decisive step in the direction of a parliamentary system reasonably similar to the British version. Clearly, however, this process can be successful only to the extent that the majority system succeeds in recreating the redeeming features characteristic of the party system of the Third Republic. One might argue that, in that case, a semi-presidential system would not be necessary; a man emerging as much the leader of a relatively homogeneous majority as Herriot did in 1924 and Blum in 1936, would hardly need more than an effective right of dissolution in order to infuse the necessary discipline into his majority. Also, it would perhaps be wiser not to designate a coalition's candidate for the position of prime minister before the election. In the two cases mentioned the office went to the leader of the strongest group within the majority, and the identity of this group might not be known beforehand.

Still, if any move is to be made to provide French government with a plebiscitary basis by direct action rather than letting this come about as a natural outgrowth of a more coherent party system, Professor Duverger's plan is the most flexible. To elect a president on the American model would mean moving farther away from the realities of French politics. The President of the United States has not always been able to exercise effective and continuous leadership, but when he has done so one of the reasons was that Congress never contained any sizable group of members who could have been called "radical" in the sense of Europe's Communists and Fascists. Congress has always been dominated by men close to the middle of the road, among whom it has, particularly in recent years, been comparatively easy for a president with the will and the ability to lead to secure a majority for the most important measures. If, however, a popularly-elected French president should have to contend with a parliament as divided as Professor Vedel assumes that it will be, he could not easily make a coherent policy prevail.

It follows, then, that if France is to find a truly institutional solution for her problems, all efforts should be concentrated on the development of a reasonably effective party system. Reference has been made repeatedly to the institutions which could help to shape it; a majority system of voting made more consistent by gradually tightening up the conditions for admission to, and the eventual abolition of, the second ballot; a right of dissolution available at any time; finally, it would seem, readmission of the possibility of simultaneous membership in the government and in parliament.

Whatever is done, the goal of true institutional stability will not be reached automatically. In 1959 everything seemed to drift in a political vacuum, with party leaders, inside and outside parliament, acting as if all they had to do was to fight for their old privileges. One may sympathize with them because the authority of parliament has been lowered more than was necessary. But, then, while Prime Minister Debré may have been wrong in the choice of some of the methods by which he wanted to assimilate French parliamentarism to the British pattern, the goal itself should not have been questioned. Slower and somewhat gentler methods may be needed, but it is essential for French parliament that it accept a position as an *intermediate* organ of government, with an executive more or less directly selected by the people themselves, and a clear position of leadership in regard to legislative as well as to executive matters.

If the path to such a goal is likely to be both long and rocky there is still a difference between knowing where one wants to go and just drifting down the path of least resistance, as was the custom during the two preceding republics. The Constitution of the Fifth Republic has, at least, managed to break with the "immobilism" of the past, and it has been guided by a government which has accomplished much that is likely to be of lasting value. To adapt its pattern of political action to the requirements of long-term stability[145] should, if the task is undertaken with a knowledge of its implications, be easier than it was to reform the Third and Fourth Republics.

FOOTNOTES

1. *Wirtschaft und Gesellschaft,* Vol. II (Tuebingen 1925), pp. 753 ff.

2. "Sense de la Grandeur Française," *Les Cahiers Politiques,* April 1944, and "Le Problème Politique Français," *ibid.*

3. For details see Institut National de la Statistique et des Etudes Economiques, *Mouvement Economique en France de 1944 à 1958* (Paris 1958). This report ends with a critical analysis (pp. 313 ff.) which emphasizes that, while economic progress is great when the figures for 1957 are compared with those for 1938, it is less great if 1929 is chosen as the basis for comparison. In particular, consumption per individual increased but little between 1929 and 1957.

4. Sirius, *Le Suicide de la Quatrième République* (Paris 1958).

5. *Journal Officiel de la République Française,* Débats Parlementaires, Assemblée National, June 2, 1958, p. 2577.

6. *The Federalist,* Modern Library edn. (New York 1937), pp. 405-7. The author is either Alexander Hamilton or James Madison. Hamilton pursues the same topic in No. 71, pp. 463 ff.

7. The troubled history of these efforts has been related in Arnold Zurcher, *The Struggle to Unite Europe, 1940-1958* (New York 1958). See, in particular, the chronicle of the European Defense Community on pp. 81 ff.

8. Maurice Duverger, *The French Political System* (Chicago 1958), pp. 186-7. For the specific problems of a caretaker government see Henry Giniger, "Interim Government Carries On in France; Caretaker Government Directs Routine Functions but Cannot Act in Big Policy Issues; Delay is Proving Costly," *The New York Times,* April 27, 1958.

9. *Politics,* Bk. III, Ch. 11.

10. *The Limitations of the Expert* (London 1931).

11. Ferdinand A. Hermens, *The Representative Republic* (Notre Dame, Ind., 1958), pp. 269-73; 285-86. For the events in Tunisia and Morocco see Herbert Luethy, "De Gaulle: Man of Destiny," *The New Leader,* August 4-11, 1959, and: Herbert Luethy, *France Against Itself,* (New York 1955), pp. 268-74.

12. For the futility of this measure, see Maurice Duverger, "Qui Est Responsable?" *Le Monde,* weekly edn., February 6-12, 1958.

13. "Le Président de la République a dit Samedi à Strasbourg," *Le Figaro,* weekly edn. of July 12, 1957.

14. Here quoted from *Time* Magazine, October 31, 1955, p. 19.

15. *La République des Camarades* (Paris 1914).

16. For the political thought of both, see Maurras' *Enqête sur la Monarchie,* first published in 1900 and 1901, definitive edition Paris 1925. The political vituperation in which they engaged culminated in the articles published in the daily, *L'Action Francaise.*

17. "350 Ministres!" *Le Figaro,* July 3, 1953.

18. Constantin Melnik and Nathan Leites, *The House Without Windows: France Selects a President* (Evanston, Ill., 1958), pp. 239 ff.

19. (Paris 1958).

20. *Op. cit.,* pp. 24-5.

21. Arthur Taylor Prescott, *Drafting the Federal Constitution* (Baton Rouge 1941).

22. *The Federalist,* No. 23, Modern Library edn., p. 143.

23. Here quoted from John Fiske, *The Critical Period of American History, 1783-1789* (Boston and New York 1888), p. 58.

24. *Ibid.*

25. *Ibid.*

26. "Today and Tomorrow," *The New York Herald Tribune,* December 8, 1953.

27. The World's Classics edn., pp. 297-8.

28. For the reasons see Hermens, *The Representative Republic,* pp. 277-8.

29. *The Federalist,* No. 71, Modern Library edn., p. 466.

30. *Les Constitutions de la France* (Paris 1946), p. 94.

31. *Political Reconstruction* (New York 1946), p. 123.

32. For the details see Peter Campbell, *French Electoral Systems and Elections, 1789-1957* (London 1958), pp. 128-9.

33. Maurice Duverger, *Political Parties* (Boston and New York 1954), pp. 216 ff.

34. *The State* (Boston 1902), pp. 221-2.

35. René Capitant, *La Reforme du Parlementarisme Français* (Paris 1934), p. 23.

36. Fernand Robert, "Une Innovation Urgente: Créer le Régime Parlementaire," *La Revue Socialiste,* April 1955.

37. Hermens, *The Representative Republic,* pp. 279-83.

38. Gordon Wright, *The Reshaping of French Democracy* (New York 1948). For a more recent, and more comprehensive, discussion see Nicholas Wahl, "Aux Origines de la Nouvelle Constitution," *Revue Française de Science Politique,* March 1959, pp. 30 ff.

39. For the text see "Le Projet de Constitution du Comité Général d'Etudes, *Les Cahiers Politiques,* October 1945.

40. *L'Année* 1944-1945, Preface d'André Siegfried (Paris 1946), pp. 292-4 and 492. These elections are, for various reasons (Hermens, *The Representative Republic,* pp. 295; 541-2) not entirely comparable to national elections, but they do, in rough outline, show how the results of majority voting differ from those of P.R.

41. J.-L. Quermonne, "Réforme des institutions et rupture de l'immobilisme," *Revue d'Action Populaire,* July-August 1958, p. 785.

42. For a convenient summary see Jean Griot, "Les différents projets de révision," *Fédération,* issue of August-September 1955, pp. 567. This issue also contains articles by leading proponents of constitutional reform such as Paul Reynaud and Professors Marcel Prélot and Georges Vedel. See also the literature on the proposal to establish presidential government cited in Hermens, *The Representative Republic,* p. 545, notes 74 and 76.

43. Maurice Duverger, *The French Political System* (Chicago 1958) p. 35.

44. Weekly edition for the period of March 20-26, 1958.

45. *Parliament* (New York 1940), p. 119.

46. *Journal Officiel,* Débats Parlementaires, Session of January 31, 1946, p. 742.

47. Robert C. Doty, "French 'Crisis System,'" *The New York Times*, May 10, 1958.

48. See, for example, the article by André Siegfried, entitled "Une Certaine Droite," *Le Figaro*, weekly edn. of April 4, 1958.

49. *Ces Princes Qui Nous Government*, (Paris 1958).

50. *La Prochaine République Sera-t-elle Républicaine?* (Paris 1958), p. xiii.

51. *Le Malaise de l'Armée* (Paris 1958).

52. "L'Armée, La Nation et Le Régime," *Le Monde*, weekly edn. for the period from February 20-26, 1958.

53. For details see Alain de Sérigny, *La Révolution du 13 Mai* (Paris 1958); Raymond Dronne, *La Révolution d'Alger* (Paris 1958). These two books are written by partisans. A more objective, if rather sensational, study has been provided by Merry and Serge Bromberger, *Les 13 Complots du 13 Mai* (Paris 1959).

54. C. L. Sulzberger. "No More Fishing in the French Rubicon," *The New York Times*, March 15, 1958.

55. *Ibid.*

56. *Ibid.*

57. For the text see *Le Monde* of May 20 and *The New York Times* of May 21, 1958.

58. *The New York Times*, March 15, 1958.

59. Henry Giniger, "Interim Government Carries on in France," *The New York Times*, April 27, 1959.

60. United Press dispatch, here quoted from *The South Bend Tribune* of April 16, 1958, published under the heading, "Nation Faces Chaos with Worst Crisis."

61. C. L. Sulzberger, "Shouting or Shooting at the Wake?" *The New York Times*, May 8, 1958.

62. *Le Monde*, weekly edn. for March 6-12, 1958.

63. For details of the debates on the vote of the plenary powers and of the revision of Art. 90, see: *Journal Officiel de la République Francaise*, Débats Parlementaires, Assemblée Nationale, issue of June 5.

64. *Ces Princes Qui Nous Government*, pp. 164 ff.

65. The text of the report was published in *Journal Officiel de la République Française*, issue of August 20, 1958, pp. 7739 ff. *Le Monde* of September 6, 1958, contains the final version of the constitution compared with the earlier draft. The details of the discussions which took place in various bodies before the new constitution was adopted have, so far, not been made public. What is known is related by François Goguel in "L'Elaboration des institutions de la République dans la Constitution du 4 Octobre 1958," *Revue Française de Science Politique*, March 1959, pp. 67 ff.

66. See, in particular, the analyses by Maurice Duverger, Georges Vedel, and Emile Giraud, published in *Le Monde*, July and August, 1958. Duverger summarized his views in his book, *Demain la République* (Paris 1958). Marcel Prélot, who had been the leading Gaullist member of the National Assembly elected in 1951, and was to become a U.N.R. Senator in 1959, expressed him-

self not uncritically on the new constitution in a series of articles in the daily, *La Croix*, which were published in book form under the title, *Pour Comprendre la Nouvelle Constitution* (Paris 1959). There is an equal undertone of criticism in the preface which René Capitant contributed to Léon Hamon, *De Gaulle dans la République* (Paris 1958).

67. *La Reforme du Parlementarisme* (Paris 1934), pp. 20-1.

68. *Ibid.*, p. 23.

69. He expressed this view in particular in a speech delivered before the Council of State on August 27, which was printed as pamphlet under the title, *La Nouvelle Constitution* (Paris 1958); see pp. 10-11.

69a. For the text see the appendix of René Capitant, *Pour Une Constitution Fédérale*, (Paris 1946), pp. 59 ff. Capitant's book has been generally regarded an an authoritative commentary on the constitutional views set forth by General de Gaulle in Bayeux.

70. During the Third and Fourth Republics the title of the chief of government had been "President of the Council of Ministers." The title "Premier" was first used in Debré's wartime draft of a new constitution.

71. Jean Châtelain, *La Nouvelle Constitution et la Régime Politique de la France* (Paris 1959), pp. 73-4.

72. "Secrets of Marly," issue of March 7, 1959, p. 853.

73. For the text see *The New York Times*, January 9, p. 3, and *Le Monde*, January 9.

74. *Le Monde*, March 27, 1959.

75. "Les Institutions de la Cinquième République," *Revue Française de Science Politique*, March 1959, p. 114.

76. *La Nouvelle Constitution*, p. 17.

77. See the book under this title by Lindsay Rogers (New York 1934); Clinton Rossiter, *Constitutional Dictatorship* (Princeton 1948); F. M. Watkins, "The Problem of Constitutional Dictatorship," in *Public Policy*, eds. Friedrich and Mason (Cambridge, Mass. 1940).

78. Maurice Duverger, "Les Institutions . . . , *op. cit.*, p. 114.

79. Jean Châtelain, *La Nouvelle Constitution*, pp. 75-6.

80. Marcel Prélot, *Pour Comprendre* . . . , p. 63. See also C. J. Friedrich, "The New French Constitution in Political and Historical Perspective," *Harvard Law Review*, March 1959, pp. 822-3.

81. "Vers Une Nouvelle Orientation de la Révision Constitutionelle?" *Revue Française de Science Politique*, July-September 1956.

82. "Under the Third and Fourth Republics the overthrow of governments was the major objective of the parliamentary game. As soon as the cabinet was formed one began to prepare for its successor. Since the average deputy had one chance out of four or five to obtain a post in the cabinet, the opening of a crisis represented for him a reasonable opportunity to realize his dream." ("Le Nouveau Parlement," *Le Monde*, April 29, 1959.)

83. *The English Constitution*, p. 164.

84. *La Mort de l'Etat Républicain* (Paris 1947), p. 98.

85. *Le Monde*, January 10, 1959.

87. For details see Châtelain, op. cit., pp. 270-2.

88. See, for example, Pierre Viansson-Ponté, "Les Damoiseaux," *Le Monde*, Octobre 14, 1958.

88a. Nicholas Wahl, "The French Constitution of 1958: The Initial Draft and Its Origins," *The American Political Science Review*, June 1959, p. 367.

89. For others see Maurice Duverger, *La V*e *République* (Paris 1959), p. 18.

90. Substitutes may ordinarily be relied upon to vote for a cabinet to which the deputy or senator belongs whom they replaced, but there is no legal obligation for them to do so.

91. *La Nouvelle Constitution . . .* , p. 9

92. *Parliament*, p. 23. Quoted by permission of the Macmillan Co.

93. *La Nouvelle Constitution . . .* , p. 9.

94. "Signification du Réferendum," *Le Figaro*, weekly edn., October 10, 1958.

95. This may also be the opinion of Maurice Duverger who refers to the incompatibility between membership in the government and in Parliament in these terms: "This innovation, detrimental as it is to the extent it diminishes the contact between the government and the assemblies, which is essential in a parliamentary system, is excellent as a means to transform the manners of the elected, and to deliver them from the psychosis of the permanent crisis." ("Le Nouveau Parlement," *Le Monde*, April 29, 1959).

96. They are set forth in Châtelain, *op. cit.*, pp. 100-124.

97. For the details see Châtelain, *op. cit.*, pp. 116-18.

98. Maurice Duverger, "Le Nouveau Sénat," *Le Monde*, April 24, 1959.

99. The ordinance of November 7, 1958 (text in Châtelain, pp. 386 ff.) adds the Economic and Social Council.

100. For the term see Friedrich, *op. cit.* The details are discussed by Châtelain, pp. 160-5.

101. Hermens, *The Representative Republic*, pp. 406-8.

102. *Ibid.*, pp. 358-60. For critical details see, among others, Guenther Willms, "Zur Reform des Bundeverfassungsgerichts," *Deutsche Richterzeitung*, June 1955.

103. "The Government and Politics of Germany" in James T. Shotwell, ed., *Governments of Continental Europe*, rev. edn. (New York 1952), p. 585.

104. F. A. Hermens, "Functional Autonomy after World War II," in Arnold Zurcher, ed., *Constitutions and Constitutional Trends Since World War II*, 2nd edn., (New York 1955), pp. 116 ff.

105. Professor Prélot (*op. cit.*, p. 41) considers it probable that there will be no dissolution until at least two governments are placed in a minority, the third then presiding over the new elections. In this case it would, indeed, be easy for "government by assembly" to return.

106. *Verfassung and Verfassungrecht*, here quoted from *Staatrechtliche Abhandlungen* (Berlin 1955), pp. 35-6.

107. *Premiers Combats pour la Constitution* (Strassbourg 1945), pp. 25 ff.

108. For the text see "Le Projet de Constitution du Comité Général d'Etudes," *Les Cahiers Politiques*, October 1945.

109. *La Mort de l'Etat Républicain*, p. 194.

110. *Ibid.*

111. Guy Mollet stated after the elections that he had advocated the majority system only in deference to the wishes of his party.

112. "Le Général de Gaulle souhaite une systeme électoral simple et clair," *Le Monde,* October 8, 1958.

113. For the text of the "ordinance" of October 13, 1958, which laid down the rules for the election of the National Assembly, see Châtelain, pp. 426 ff.

114. "Campagne couteuse pour 435 candidats," *Le Figaro,* November 28, 1958.

115. This was pointed out in detail in Helmut Unkelbach, *Grundlagen der Wahlsystematik: Stabilitaetsbedingungen der parlamentarischen Demokratie* (Goettingen 1956).

116. The same applies to the plurality system. During the Third Republic, opponents of plurality voting would (quite rightly) tell its proponents: "Ce n'est pas le second tour du scrutin que vous voulez supprimer; c'est le premier." "It is not the second ballot that you want to suppress; it is the first."

117. Peter Campbell, *French Electoral Systems and Elections, 1789-1957* (London 1958), p. 126.

118. *Élections Législatives, Résultats Officiels* (Paris 1936), p. vi.

119. As already mentioned the "popular front" of 1936 was something quite different from more recent ventures under the same name. For details, see Hermens, *Democracy or Anarchy?,* pp. 125-140.

120. Marcel Gabilly, "Tactique électorale uniforme: celle du 'chacun pour soi,'" *Le Figaro,* weekly edn. of October 24, 1958.

121. For some details see J. Blondel, "The French General Election of November 1958," *Parliamentary Affairs,* Winter 1958-59; Marcel Merle, "Du referendum aux élections législatives," *Revue d'Action Populaire,* January 1959: René Rémond, "Le nouveau régime et les forces politiques," *Revue Française de Science Politique* (March 1959).

122. *Le Monde* of December 2.

123. Jean-Jacques Servan-Schreiber, analyzing the results of the first ballot in the November 27 issue of the weekly, *L'Express,* tried to show that the entire vote was more Pétainist than Gaullist. He pointed out that almost everywhere a Gaullist of the Right beat a Gaullist of the Left, and that, in addition, a candidate of the Right who was at all known to the voters would beat even a Gaullist of the Right. This picture is overdrawn; what is significant in the long run is the intention of the voters, and where they went rather far to the Right they did so, for the most part, in order to give emphatic support to what they considered the intentions of General de Gaulle.

124. "Si la Représentation proportionnelle avait joué . . . ," *Le Monde,* December 6, 1958.

125. The term was used by Etienne Fajon, "Le Blé qui Lévera," *L'Humanite,* December 2, 1958.

126. René Andrieu, "Premiéres Constatations," issue of November 24, 1958.

127. Issue of December 2, 1958.

128. For details see Raymond Aron, "La Ve République choisit la rigueur monétaire," *Preuves,* May 1959 and J. L. Fyot: "La France prend une nouvelle orientation économique," *Revue d'Action Populaire,* February 1959.

129. *Le Monde* of February 17, February 24, and March 4. The issues of February 17 and March 3 contain comments by Jacques Fauvet on the rise of the Communist vote.

130. *Le Monde*, February 25, 1959.

131. Results were published in *Le Monde* of March 10 and 17.

132. For details see *Bilans Politiques, Economiques et Sociaux,* issue of March 12.

133. *Le Monde*, March 18. 1959.

134. "Les listes de front populaire," *Le Monde*, March 18, 1959.

135. *Le Monde* of April 29, 1958; this issue also contains the results of the voting in each department.

136. We follow the election results as given by the Ministry of the Interior. The actual composition of the groups within the Senate is different: U.N.R. 34 members, Independents 68, Group of Rural Action 20, Democratic and Radical Left 48, M.R.P. 33, Socialists 51, Communists 14, others 5. This enumeration excludes states from the former colonies which became members of the Community. See: "Le Sénat de la Ve République," *Revue Politique des Idées et des Institutions,* April 15/30, 1959, pp. 233-236.

137. *Ibid.*

138. "Un homme a remplacé l'Etat," *La Nef,* May 1959.

139. W. Ivor Jennings, *Parliament,* pp. 91 ff.

140. For an exception see George Vedel, "La Pratique des Ordres du Jour," *Le Monde,* May 7, 1959. Professor Vedel took the view that whatever was not explicitly forbidden by the constitution was allowed. On the other hand, all the government would have to do in order to avoid being embarrassed by undesirable votes was to have one of its friends move "the passage pure and simple to the remainder of the agenda." Such a motion had always an absolute priority and the government could then "engage its responsibility" according to Art. 49 of the constitution. In that case there would be no vote unless the opposition should introduce a motion of censure and carry it with a majority of the Assembly's membership.

141. Maurice Duverger, "Deux Mois de Chambre Introuvable," *Le Monde,* June 21 and 22, 1959.

142. Raymond Aron, "La Démocratie a-t-elle un avenir en France," published in *Preuves* for August 1959, spoke for the latter when he wrote: "We do not know the outcome of this future battle (between parliament and government) but at least a negative prediction seems incontestable: The combination of an executive in the style of Louis XIV with a parliament submitted to English discipline by M. Michel Debré is impossible in the long run."

143. Crosby S. Noyes, "Army's Loyalty Holds Key to a Universal Question," *The Washington Star,* October 1958.

144. For details, see Hermens, *The Representative Republic,* pp. 318 ff., and for the bibliography, Footnote 74 on p. 545.

145. Much depends, of course, on the solution of the Algerian problem. On this point as well as on others see: Karl Loewenstein, "The Constitution of the Fifth Republic, A Preliminary Report," *The Journal of Politics,* 1959, pp. 211 ff., in particular p. 232. See also Georges Vedel, "Verité de la Ve Répub-

lique," *Revue de l'Action Populaire,* Sept.-Oct. 1959. On the constitution as a whole, see also Stanley H. Hoffmann, "The French Constitution of 1958: The Final Text and Its Prospects," *The American Political Science Review,* June 1959, pp. 355-6.

UNIVERSITY OF NOTRE DAME PRESS PUBLICATIONS

BOLSHEVISM: AN INTRODUCTION TO SOVIET COM-
MUNISM, Waldemar Gurian $3.25

CATHOLICISM, NATIONALISM AND DEMOCRACY IN
ARGENTINA, John J. Kennedy 4.75

CHRISTIAN DEMOCRACY IN ITALY AND FRANCE,
Mario Einaudi and François Goguel 4.00

CHRISTIAN DEMOCRACY IN WESTERN EUROPE, Mi-
chael P. Fogarty 6.75

DIPLOMACY IN A CHANGING WORLD, eds. Stephen D.
Kertesz and M. A. Fitzsimons 7.50

DIPLOMACY IN A WHIRLPOOL: HUNGARY BETWEEN
NAZI GERMANY AND SOVIET RUSSIA, ed. Stephen D.
Kertesz 4.75

THE FATE OF EAST CENTRAL EUROPE: HOPES AND
FAILURES OF AMERICAN FOREIGN POLICY ed. Ste-
phen D. Kertesz 6.25

THE FOREIGN POLICY OF THE BRITISH LABOUR GOV-
ERNMENT, 1945-1951, M. A. Fitzsimons 3.25

FREEDOM AND REFORM IN LATIN AMERICA, Fredrick
B. Pike 6.00

GERMAN PROTESTANTS FACE THE SOCIAL QUES-
TION, William Shanahan 6.75

INTRODUCTION TO MODERN POLITICS, Ferdinand A.
Hermens 3.50

PAN-SLAVISM: ITS HISTORY AND IDEOLOGY, Hans Kohn 6.25

THE REPRESENTATIVE REPUBLIC, Ferdinand A. Hermens 7.50

THE RUSSIAN REVOLUTION AND RELIGION, 1917-
1925, Boleslaw Szczesniak 6.75

SOVIET IMPERIALISM: ITS ORIGINS AND TACTICS, ed.
Waldemar Gurian 3.75

SOVIET POLICY TOWARD THE BALTIC STATES, 1918-
1940, Albert N. Tarulis 5.50

THEORETICAL ASPECTS OF INTERNATIONAL RELA-
TIONS, ed. William T. R. Fox 3.25

WHAT AMERICA STANDS FOR, eds. Stephen D. Kertesz
and M. A. Fitzsimons 4.75

WHY DEMOCRACIES FAIL: A CRITICAL EVALUATION
OF THE CAUSES FOR MODERN DICTATORSHIPS,
Norman L. Stamps 4.00

UNIVERSITY OF NOTRE DAME PRESS, Notre Dame, Indiana

Index of Names

89